Lecture Notes of the Institute for Computer Sciences, Social Informatics and Telecommunications Engineering 190

Nathalie Mitton · Hakima Chaouchi
Thomas Noel · Thomas Watteyne
Alban Gabillon · Patrick Capolsini (Eds.)

Interoperability, Safety and Security in IoT

Second International Conference, InterIoT 2016
and Third International Conference, SaSeIoT 2016
Paris, France, October 26–27, 2016
Revised Selected Papers

 Springer

Editors

Nathalie Mitton
Inria Lille-Nord Europe
Villeneuve d' Ascq
France

Hakima Chaouchi
Telecom Sud Paris
Evry
France

Thomas Noel
University of Strasbourg
Illkirch
France

Thomas Watteyne
INRIA-Paris
Paris
France

Alban Gabillon
French Polynesian University
Faa'a
French Polynesia

Patrick Capolsini
University of French Polynesia
Faa'a
French Polynesia

ISSN 1867-8211   ISSN 1867-822X   (electronic)
Lecture Notes of the Institute for Computer Sciences, Social Informatics
and Telecommunications Engineering
ISBN 978-3-319-52726-0   ISBN 978-3-319-52727-7   (eBook)
DOI 10.1007/978-3-319-52727-7

Library of Congress Control Number: 2017931539

Printed on acid-free paper

This Springer imprint is published by Springer Nature
The registered company is Springer International Publishing AG
The registered company address is: Gewerbestrasse 11, 6330 Cham, Switzerland

Preface

InterIoT

After a successful first edition in Rome, it was our great pleasure to welcome attendees to the Second EAI International Conference on Interoperability in IoT in Paris, France. Colocated with SaseIoT 2016, InterIoT 2016 displayed an exciting technical program consisting of one keynote speech and technical sessions that presented original and fundamental research advances on all aspects of interoperability of these heterogeneous IoT platforms. Indeed, IoT products are now hitting the market across a large variety of segments. Often driven by the fear to "fall behind," small and large companies push their engineering teams to produce solutions quickly. The result is that the market is highly fragmented: A large number of non-interoperable solutions are being installed, eventually leading to increased cost, inefficiencies, customer frustration, and a rate of adoption of the IoT much slower than the numbers touted by analysts. The market is now at a state where we need to think about interoperability. Interoperability appears to a major and new challenge.

The goal of InterIoT is to bring together practicing engineers and advanced researchers to share the state of the art around interoperability in the IoT, analyze what is needed, and identify the work that lies ahead to increase the number of interoperable IoT products.

We received high-quality submissions from all parts of the world. After a rigorous review process, eight regular papers were included in the technical program. The program also featured a keynote address by Prof. Manfred Hauswirth, director of the Fraunhofer Institute for Open Communication Systems, Germany.

We would like to gratefully thank our publicity and web chair, Dr. Miguel Elias Mitre Campista from UFRJ, Brazil, who made a remarkable job in the establishment of the technical program and in the communication. It would have not been possible without the help of all the Technical Program Committee members and external reviewers who volunteered their time and professional expertise. We would like to take this opportunity to thank all of them for their help. We would also like to thank all the authors for contributing their quality work, and our sponsors and partners for their support, including CREATE-NET and EAI. We received excellent support from our sponsors, especially from Anna Horvathova, who managed conference organization. Sincere thanks to her.

December 2016

Nathalie Mitton
Thomas Noel
Thomas Watteyne

SaSeIoT

The Third EAI International Conference on Safety and Security in Internet of Things (SaSeIoT' 2016) was held in Paris, France, on October 27, 2016 in conjunction with InterIoT 2016 conference.

This international conference attracted submissions from various countries. Each paper went through a rigorous peer-review process, with each submission receiving multiple reviews from the members of the Technical Program Committee. We could only select a few of the highest-quality papers for inclusion in the final program.

The accepted papers, which focus on security, safety, and privacy issues, provide great insight into the latest research findings in the area of Internet of Things. In addition to the technical papers, the workshop program also included one keynote speech on "Privacy Issue in Internet of Things" by Dr. Gilad Rosner from the Internet of Things Privacy Forum.

We would like to thank all the people who worked hard to make this conference a real success. First and foremost, we thank all authors who submitted their papers for consideration as well as all Technical Program Committee members for their time in providing rigorous, timely reviews. We would also like to thank European Alliance for Innovation (EAI) for its sponsorship.

December 2016   Hakima Chaouchi
                                                      Alban Gabillon
                                                      Patrick Capolsini

Organization

InterIoT Organizing Committee

General Chair

Nathalie Mitton · Inria, France

General Co-chair

Thomas Noel · University of Strasbourg, France

Technical Program Committee Chair

Thomas Watteyne · Inria, France

Web Chair, Publicity and Social Media Chair, Publications Chair

Miguel Elias Mitre Campista · Universidade Federal do Rio de Janeiro, Brazil

Sponsorship and Exhibits Chair

Nathalie Mitton · Inria, France

Local Chair

Thomas Watteyne · Inria, France

Conference Manager

Anna Horváthová · European Alliance for Innovation

SaSeIoT Organizing Committee

General Chair

Hakima Chaouchi · EIT ICT Labs, Institut Mines Telecom-Telecom Sud Paris

Technical Program Committee Chair

Alban Gabillon   University of French Polynesia

Sponsorship and Exhibits Chair

Hakima Chaouchi   EIT ICT Labs, Institut Mines Telecom-Telecom Sud Paris,
                             France

Tutorials Chair

Patrick Capolsini   University of French Polynesia

Website Chair

Anna Horváthová   European Alliance for Innovation, Slovak Republic

Conference Manager

Anna Horváthová   European Alliance for Innovation

Contents

InterIoT

Comparative Analysis of Opportunistic Communication Technologies

Jens Dede[✉] and Anna Förster

Sustainable Communication Networks, University of Bremen, Bremen, Germany
{jd,afoerster}@comnets.uni-bremen.de
http://www.comnets.uni-bremen.de

Abstract. Opportunistic or device-to-device communications offer a great chance for straight-forward and cost-effective interoperability among various devices and manufacturers, from tiny sensors to end-used smartphones. However, their implementation is not trivial, as no standard communication technologies exist for their purposes. This paper explores the available options, qualitatively compares their properties, focusing especially on power consumption and user friendliness. We also offer an experimental comparison of their energy consumption and discuss further needed developments.

Keywords: Opportunistic Networks · Bluetooth · BLE · WiFi · Internet of Things · IoT · Interoperability · Energy consumption

1 Introduction

In recent years, our daily use of electronic devices and the Internet changed dramatically. The massive increase in smartphone usage and the ever increasing coverage with high-speed Internet services have affected the way we work and live. The vision of all devices around us connected and cooperating with each other for the sake of our comfort or a more sustainable lifestyle is getting closer.

Almost all of nowadays communication-based services require a network connection and a central processing point and thus infrastructure. However, there are several scenarios which have to work without a connection. Either, the infrastructure is not available due to missing coverage, overload or a disaster or the user is not willing to use it. As a result, research emerged on infrastructure-less communication mainly referred to as Opportunistic Networks (OppNets) or opportunistic services. Much effort has been invested by researchers in understanding how data dissemination works in these environments and how to ensure certain quality of service. These services are also highly interesting for the Internet of Things (IoT), as they offer interoperability among various manufacturers and systems. All they need is a common format for exchanging data and a common communication interface. The biggest advantage is that they offer a direct and geographically localized interface between the "things" such as sensors or actuators and the end users. Thus, opportunistic services could become one of

© ICST Institute for Computer Sciences, Social Informatics and Telecommunications Engineering 2017
N. Mitton et al. (Eds.): InterIoT 2016/SaSeIot 2016, LNICST 190, pp. 3–10, 2017.
DOI: 10.1007/978-3-319-52727-7_1

the driving factors of the IoT. However, data dissemination and quality of service are still under research, which needs active cooperation from real users. Motivating users is probably the main non-technical challenge in this area.

Developing real world OppNets is not trivial, though. Since there is no standard or semi-standard communication technology, especially designed for OppNets, developers have started using existing technologies in non-usual ways or are extending them. However, our own experience [2] have taught us that most of the solutions are not optimal and trade-offs are the rule.

This paper compares all broadly available communication technologies for OppNets. We explicitly focus on two of their properties: user friendliness and energy consumption. More concretely, we offer:

1. A concise survey of existing technologies and their uses for implementing opportunistic services for end-user devices (smartphones) in Sect. 2
2. A qualitative comparison of their properties and technical details in Sect. 3
3. An experimental comparison of their energy consumption in Sect. 4

2 Background and Related Works

The most widespread end-user device is nowadays the smartphone. Other IoT devices, are left out of the scope, since they usually provide researchers with more flexibility for implementation than end-user devices. Thus, in this study, we explore the usage of a smartphone for testing and evaluating OppNets.

Mainly two technologies are used for implementing OppNets: WiFi and Bluetooth and their variants. They are both available on most smartphone platforms.

WiFi or IEEE 802.11 is being used in three different variants: traditional WiFi, WiFi direct and WiFi ad hoc. The ad hoc mode is deprecated and not available on Android and iOS, unless the phones are rooted or jailbroken. In WiFi direct, one phone acts as an access point (AP), the other as a client. Several technologies like service discovery are used to ease the usage. The traditional WiFi consists of APs and clients whereas nowadays smartphones can act as both. The authors in [10] use WiFi APs to transmit data in an opportunistic way between the nodes. They use static APs as well as mobile phones acting so. The authors in [13] suggest an ad hoc networking model designed for Bluetooth Low Energy (BLE), WiFi and classic Bluetooth. An implementation using WiFi SSIDs is provided. The opportunistic short message service introduced in [12] is also based on a WiFi SSIDs for transmitting the data and has been evaluated with 20 smartphones.

Bluetooth or IEEE 802.15.1 exists in two different variants: traditional Bluetooth (before 4.0) and Bluetooth Low Energy (BLE, 4.0 and up). BLE has been designed for low power consumption and is currently available on most modern smartphones and on some IoT platforms. A device discovery protocol for Bluetooth 2.1 was introduced in [5]. In there, the authors also measure the energy consumption of their approach and compare WiFi to Bluetooth on Nokia

N900 Smartphones. *bCards@PerCom—2012*[1] is an Android app for exchanging business cards during conferences. It uses Bluetooth to detect proximity but the contact details are exchanged using a central server. A wireless mesh protocol for IPv6 is introduced in [7] where the authors use the Generic Access Profile (GAP) (BLE advertisements) which was introduced in Bluetooth 4.0.

Hybrid approaches combine WiFi and Bluetooth for communication. The authors in [8] use WiFi and Bluetooth to detect proximity and use this data to determine whether opportunistic communication is feasible. In [11], the authors compare the energy consumption of their OppNet application with WiFi and BLE. In some way, this resembles the work presented by us here. However, we offer an application-agnostic detailed comparison of all available technologies.

Using OppNets to offload data from 3G mobile networks is suggested in [4]. Valuable work on the energy consumption of the different technologies was provided, but unfortunately the explored technologies are deprecated.

There are also **frameworks** for opportunistic communications, such as Google's Nearby[2] and Apple's *Multipeer Connectivity Framework*[3]. However, Nearby requires Internet connection and internally uses a central server to establish the connection. Thus, it cannot be used for truly OppNets. Apple's Multipeer framework as introduced in iOS 7 allows to connect two devices without an Internet connection. To achieve this, it uses a combination of WiFi and BLE. Unfortunately, it is proprietary and only available on iOS.

To the best of our knowledge, FireChat [9] is the only application which supports real infrastructureless communication. They use Apple's Multipeer framework for inter iOS communication and a combination of WiFi and BLE for the communication between Android phones and Android and iOS phones.

As already mentioned above, the main goal of most of the above publications is the research on OppNets, not their implementation. However, the concrete implementation has a great impact on the achieved results (e.g. user motivation to use the service, number of users targeted, etc.). For example, some of the implementations impact the normal usage of WiFi networks, which is uncomfortable for the users. Others severely impact the power consumption of the smartphones and leaves the user without power in the middle of a busy day. In the next section, we will compare these technologies and their variants in terms of their technical details, properties and usability.

3 Comparison of the Technologies

Table 1 gives an overview of the considered technologies and their variants, as identified in the previous section. It summarizes their options, effects and their support in the main operating systems (Android and iOS).

---

[1] play.google.com/store/apps/details?id=supsi.dti.percom

[2] developers.google.com/nearby/.

[3] developer.apple.com.

WiFi Direct. WiFi direct is mainly used by Android based phones and is not supported by iOS. It is meant for transmitting data with high data rates and does not allow the parallel usage of the WiFi interface for other purposes (e.g. browsing the web). The absolute energy consumption is high (see Sect. 4 for details). Due to security reasons, it requires user authentication for each connection, e.g. by entering a PIN, scanning a QR-code, etc.

WiFi SSID or Tethering. Almost all current smartphones can act as an **access point (AP)** (tether) and the broadcasted SSID can be used as information carrier. As a phone cannot act as an AP and scan for available APs at the same time, it has to switch between both modes to send/receive data. Meanwhile no Internet connection via WiFi is possible. According to [6], the maximum size of the SSID is 32 bytes which corresponds to the maximum amount of data transmitted and thus limits the data rate. Providing an AP and actively scanning for nearby APs requires a high amount of energy. As the data is broadcasted using the SSID, no pairing or user interaction is required.

WiFi Ad Hoc. Similarly to WiFi Direct, WiFi ad hoc supports high packet sizes and high data rates. The energy consumption is high and no parallel usage is possible (as for all WiFi based approaches). The ad hoc mode is only supported by certain rooted Android phones and not available for iOS unless they are jailbroken. As the phone has to be rooted anyway, the pairing could be adapted according to the requirements. The rooting is also the major drawback of the solution: It is not feasible for the majority of the non-technical users.

Classic Bluetooth. The classic Bluetooth starting at version 2.0 with Enhanced Data Rate (EDR) supports unlimited data sizes and a data rate of 2.1 MBit/s. The energy consumption is low compared to WiFi and pairing is required for normal operation. However, several implementations of OppNets managed to overcome the pairing using different approaches. The main trick is to allow smartphones to communicate to each other, if they are registered on the same server. This requires an Internet connection and is thus not suitable for real opportunistic communication. It is possible to use several Bluetooth connections at the same time and the standard is supported by all smartphones.

Bluetooth Low Energy. BLE is an energy optimized Bluetooth standard available since version 4.2 [1]. It is designed for energy constrained devices like smart watches and sensors. The standard offers the Generic Attribute Prole (GATT) for transmitting small amounts of data and GAP (advertisements) for broadcasts which was originally developed for location based services (beacons) on dedicated hardware. Recent iOS and Android phones support transmitting BLE beacons (Android since 5.0, iOS since iOS 7). Especially the BLE beacons seem to be ideal for OppNets as no pairing is required and the user can use other Bluetooth devices in parallel. Additionally, the energy consumption is very low.

Table 1. Qualitative comparison of technologies for OppNets

	WiFi			Bluetooth		Misc.
	Direct	Tethering	Ad Hoc[a]	classic	BLE	Multi -peer[e]
Data Size	unlimited	32 bytes	unlimited	unlimited	31 bytes	unlimited
Data Rate	high[f]	32 bytes per interval	high[f]	2.1 MBit/s[g]	31 bytes per interval	high
Energy[b]	medium to high	high	high	low	very low	depends[e]
Pairing	yes	no	no	yes[c]	no	no
Parallel usage	no	no	no	yes	yes	depends[e]
Platform	Android	Android, iOS	No[a]	Android, iOS	Android[d], iOS	iOS

[a]WiFi ad hoc requires rooting/jailbreaking the phone
[b]Concrete energy measurements are provided in Sect. 4.
[c]Some workarounds exists in combination with WiFi
[d]BLE is supported since Android 5.0 on platforms with a Bluetooth 4.2 chipset
[e]Multipeer Connectivity is a proprietary standard by Apple, only limited information available
[f]Depends on the WiFi chipset. Usually at least 54 MBit/s
[g]Bluetooth 2.0 with Enhanced Data Rate

Unfortunately, the size of one frame is quite low with a maximum of 31 bytes using raw frames and 20 bytes sticking to the beacon standard.

In the next section, the energy consumption of the variants of WiFi and Bluetooth are measured and compared.

4   Measurement of Selected Energy Consumption Profiles

In this section, the energy consumption of different technologies is monitored and compared in an application-agnostic way.

Measurement Setup. For the energy measurements an Android reference platform is used: Google's Nexus 6P [3]. It supports all required technologies, runs on Android 6 and has a 3450 mAh battery. We use a brand new phone (factory defaults). The phone has no SIM card and the cellular connection and GPS are disabled. The only installed Apps (besides Android's standard Apps) are *EnergyMonitor*[4] and *Locate Beacon*[5]. *Locate Beacon* is an example App for

---

[4] https://github.com/ComNets-Bremen/EnergyMonitor.
[5] https://play.google.com/store/apps/details?id=com.radiusnetworks.locate.

transmitting BLE beacons in Android. *EnergyMonitor* logs the battery level as percentage, the time and the charging status to an internal database.

For each experiment, the phone is fully charged, switched to the mode for the corresponding experiment and left untouched till the battery is completely drained. The side effects of charging and discharging the battery are neglected. Using this general setup, the following measurements were performed:

- **Flight mode:** The phone is switched to flight mode and no App or communication technology is used. This results in the maximum achievable battery lifetime and serves as a reference for all other measurements.
- **BLE beacons:** Only Bluetooth is enable. The App *Locate Beacon* is enabled and set to transmit beacons with the maximum transmit power and the maximum transmit interval of 10 beacons per second. This corresponds to an opportunistic communication app using BLE beacons.
- **WiFi not connected:** Only WiFi is enabled and no WiFi AP is in range. This causes the phone to scan continuously for WiFi networks.
- **WiFi connected:** This demonstrates how Android behaves if an AP is in range, as compared to no AP in range. The real energy consumption of an OppNet application would then lie somewhere between these two profiles.
- **Tethering/AP:** In this measurement, the phone acts as an AP. It transmits a WiFi SSID and offers a connection. This corresponds to the worst case energy consumption for WiFi direct and apps using SSIDs for information dissemination.
- **FireChat:** FireChat (version 7.9.9) is a well known Apps running on Android and iOS for OppNets with a notable number of users. We use it as an example app to set the other results into the context to a real world implementation.

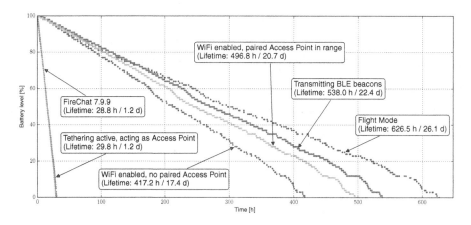

Fig. 1. Energy consumption of different communication technologies (WiFi, Bluetooth)

Measurement Results. Fig. 1 depicts the energy consumption of the different technologies. It can be seen that switching on the tethering mode on a Smartphone (i.e. turning it to an AP) increases the energy consumption significantly compared to all other applications. Acting as a WiFi client is optimized on Android and thus results into an acceptable battery lifetime. Here, a difference can be seen between the results with and without a paired AP in range: If an AP is in range, the battery lifetime is increased by 19% (496.6 h instead of 417.2 h). If no AP is in range, Android performs more WiFi scans to find a suitable network. This increases the energy consumption. Transmitting BLE beacons is highly optimized. Although we set the phone to the most energy consuming BLE mode, i.e. high transmit power, 10 beacons per second, the battery lifetime is still high and still 86% of the time achieved in flight mode.

FireChat is the only opportunistic communication app with a notable number of users. Comparing the energy consumption with the other results shows, that developers seem to use mainly WiFi to transmit data: The battery lifetime is even lower then the lifetime achieved by acting as an AP.

The graphs in Fig. 1 are almost perfectly linear besides humps at the battery level below 11% caused by the internal battery behaviour and circuits.

Discussion. Current implementations and test setups for OppNets focus on data dissemination and quality of service. The user experience is neglected by most of them. The comparison from Sect. 3 and the measurements from Sect. 4 show that the primary everyday usage is significantly effected by an opportunistic app. It acts like a secondary phone user and decreases the battery lifetime or occupies fully some services, like the WiFi connection. To achieve a meaningful spreading of these applications and to foster research on them, the negative side-effects have to be reduced to a minimum. From our results, using state-of-the-art BLE technologies, including the upcoming Bluetooth 5 seems to be suitable and the number of BLE enabled phones is constantly increasing.

Another solution might be WiFi, but security and energy issues are not to be easily resolved. We believe that WiFi based OppNets on phones will disappear.

Security is a very major challenge in OppNets. Bluetooth and especially the new Bluetooth 5 is expected to handle well security. For WiFi, this issue is not solved very well and either requires the user to authorize every single transmission or is simply disabled. This is another reason to focus on Bluetooth.

Another candidate for OppNets is IEEE 802.15.4 (ZigBee). It is widely available for IoT devices, but for almost no end-user device.

5 Conclusion and Future Work

In this paper, we performed a detailed analysis of available communication technologies for implementing OppNets. We explored their properties and user friendliness and experimentally compared their energy consumption. We came to the conclusion that state-of-the-art Bluetooth technologies are best suited for truly opportunistic services, which affect only minimally the comfort of the users.

Next we will explore the upcoming Bluetooth 5 standard. Furthermore, we will explore interoperability between smartphones and IoT devices in OppNets.

References

1. Bluetooth, SIG.: Bluetooth specification version 4.2. Bluetooth SIG (2014)
2. Foerster, A., Udugama, A., Görg, C., Kuladinithi, K., Timm-Giel, A., Cama-Pinto, A.: A novel data dissemination model for organic data flows. In: Agüero, R., Zinner, T., García-Lozano, M., Wenning, B.-L., Timm-Giel, A. (eds.) MONAMI 2015. LNICSSITE, vol. 158, pp. 239–252. Springer, Heidelberg (2015). doi:10.1007/978-3-319-26925-2_18
3. Google Inc.: Nexus 6P. www.google.com/nexus/6p/. Accessed 06, Sept 2016
4. Han, B., Hui, P., Kumar, V.S.A., Marathe, M.V., Shao, J., Srinivasan, A.: Mobile data offloading through opportunistic communications and social participation. IEEE Trans. Mob. Comput. **11**(5), 821–834 (2012)
5. Han, B., Srinivasan, A.: eDiscovery: energy efficient device discovery for mobile opportunistic communications. In: IEEE International Conference on Network Protocols, pp. 1–10 (2012)
6. IEEE: IEEE Standard for Information technology. IEEE Std 802.11-2012 (2012)
7. Kim, H.S., Lee, J., Jang, J.W.: BLEmesh: a wireless mesh network protocol for bluetooth low energy devices. In: 2015 3rd International Conference on Future Internet of Things and Cloud (FiCloud), pp. 558–563 (2015)
8. Liu, S., Striegel, A.D.: Exploring the potential in practice for opportunistic networks amongst smart mobile devices. In: Proceedings of the 19th Annual International Conference on Mobile Computing & Networking, pp. 315–326. ACM, New York (2013)
9. Open Garden: opengarden.com Accessed 07 June 2016
10. Trifunovic, S., Distl, B., Schatzmann, D., Legendre, F.: Wifi-opp: ad-hoc-less opportunistic networking. In: Proceedings of the 6th ACM Workshop on Challenged Networks, pp. 37–42. ACM (2011)
11. Turkes, O., Scholten, H., Havinga, P.J.: Blessed with opportunistic beacons: a lightweight data dissemination model for smart mobile ad-hoc networks. In: Proceedings of the ACM MobiCom Workshop on Challenged Networks, pp. 25–30 (2015)
12. Turkes, O., Scholten, H., Havinga, P.J.M.: Friend-to-friend short message service with opportunistic wi-fi beacons. In: IEEE International Conference on Pervasive Computing and Communication Workshops, pp. 1–6 (2016)
13. Turkes, O., Scholten, H., Havinga, P.J.M.: Opportunistic beacon networks: information dissemination via wireless network identifiers. In: 2016 IEEE International Conference on Pervasive Computing and Communication Workshops, pp. 1–6 (2016)

Technical Overview of F-Interop

Rémy Leone[1]([✉]), Federico Sismondi[2], Thomas Watteyne[1], and César Viho[2]

[1] Inria, EVA Team, Rennes, France
{remy.leone,thomas.watteyne}@inria.fr
[2] Irisa, Rennes, France
{federico.sismondi,cesar.viho}@irisa.fr

Abstract. Interoperability and conformance testing are needed to ensure that systems behave as specified by the standards they implement. Today, interoperability testing is done through face-to-face "interop events". Requiring physical presence of all parties impacts the scalability of the testing, and slows down the development of standards-based products.

F-Interop is a platform which enables *remote* interoperability and conformance testing of networking standards. This paper gives a technical overview of the project and its software architecture. The architecture follows the event bus design pattern: generic messages are routed between the different software components, some of these running at different locations.

Keywords: Interoperability testing · Conformance testing · Remote testing · Online · Platform

1 Introduction

F-Interop is a platform which provides remote interoperability and conformance testing of network standards. F-Interop allows to reduce the time to market of devices by providing a platform to test interoperability remotely and autonomously to find problems sooner. It also helps communities working on standards finding at an early stage potential interoperability problems in draft standards.

This paper gives a technical overview of the F-Interop platform represented, and serves as a technical companion paper to [5]. Its software architecture which will be described in detail throughout this paper.

The remainder of this paper is organized as follows. Section 2 presents current best practice and the associated limitations. Section 3 introduces the F-Interop platform with a focus on the technical architecture. Section 4 presents how a test is executed in the platform. Section 5 discusses how this architecture is suitable for many types of test cases.

© ICST Institute for Computer Sciences, Social Informatics and Telecommunications Engineering 2017
N. Mitton et al. (Eds.): InterIoT 2016/SaSeIot 2016, LNICST 190, pp. 11–17, 2017.
DOI: 10.1007/978-3-319-52727-7_2

2   Interoperability and Current Best Practice

Conformance testing determines whether a system complies to the requirements. Conformance testing is key for having interoperable implementations, but it is not enough on its own. For this reason, conformance testing is always complemented with interoperability testing. Interoperability testing focuses on end-to-end functionality between two systems/implementations implementing the same standard(s).

Both conformance and interoperability testing are based on use cases which are abstract illustrations of the typical behavior of a system. The behavior is defined in standards, a document (usually a standard or technical specification) from a recognized Standards Developing Organization (SDO). A Test Description (TD) is derived from the standard. It is a set of test cases which covers the different behavior a standard defines. The goal of conformance and interoperability tests is to run test cases, and for each generate a pass/fail verdict.

Today, interoperability events are face-to-face meetings in which vendors bring their Implementation Under Test (IUT). The TD of the event is prepared before the events and distributed to the participants. The TD contains a list of Test Cases (TC), each of them describing a particular configuration and a sequence of actions the participants need to follow. ETSI[1] has for example organized interoperability events for various low-power wireless protocols such as CoAP [1,4], 6Lo(WPAN) [2]. and 6TiSCH [3].

Figure 1 gives an simple example test case for the CoAP protocol, as specified in [1]. For this test case, one CoAP client IUT issues a CoAP GET request (the "stimuli") to a CoAP server IUT. The CoAP Server is pre-configured to

Interoperability Test Description			
Identifier:	TD_COAP_CORE_01		
Objective:	Perform GET transaction (CON mode)		
Configuration:	CoAP_CFG_01		
References:	[1] 4.4.1, 4.4.3, 5.8.1		
Pre-test conditions:	• Server offers the resource /test that handle GET with an arbitrary payload		
Test Sequence:	Step	Type	Description
	1	stimulus	Client is requested to send a GET request with: • Type = 0(CON) • Code = 1(GET)
	2	check (CON)	Sent request contains Type value indicating 0 and Code value indicating 1
	3	check (CON)	Server sends response containing: • Code = 69(2.05 Content) • The same Message ID as that of the previous request • Content type option
	4	verify (IOP)	Client displays the received information

Fig. 1. Example CoAP test case, as specified in [1].

---

[1] The European Telecommunications Standards Institute, http://www.etsi.org/.

offer resource /test. A sniffer mechanisms is required to capture the different messages exchanged. Once the CoAP transaction is over, participants then manually check the format/contents of these messages, and verify that they comply with the standards (steps 2 and 3 in Fig. 1). The test case generates a "pass" verdict if all the "check" steps pass and the users verify that their IUTs behaved correctly.

Hundreds of face-to-face interoperability events have taken place, resulting in numerous standards compliant and interoperable products to hit the market. The drawback of this approach, however, is that they are infrequent and require engineering teams to travel. Because they typically happen only every couple of months, even a small mistake in an implementation requires that team to delay product release by several. Similarly, such frequent travels might cost too much for small companies wanted to release standards-compliant products. The net result is standards-based products take longer to hit the market, and that consumers are often bound to proprietary products which are often faster and cheaper to create.

The goal of F-Interop is to make conformance and interoperability testing faster and cheaper. It does so by allowing tests to be conducted remotely and online. A server of the Internet plays the role of a "virtual room" in which vendors meet to test their IUTs. The IUT itself does not leave the vendor's premises; instead, an agent running on a computer at the vendor's connects to the server. The agent then remotely drives the IUT and goes through the different test cases. This means that a vendor can launch a conformance testing session at any time, possibly as part of its continuous integration process. Interoperability testing means that different vendors connect to the system at the same time.

3   The F-Interop Platform

Figure 2 shows the software architecture of F-Interop. The architecture is responsible for managing the testing infrastructure necessary, including provisioning the underlying network, capturing trace, starting/stopping the different tests, and reporting the verdicts. Through standard security mechanisms, the architecture ensures the authentication of the different users, and the confidentiality of test results. The following sub-sections describe the different blocks in Fig. 2.

3.1   The "Event Bus" Software Design Pattern

The F-Interop architecture is composed of different components exchanging messages through an "Event Bus". All communication is done through this mechanism, including control messages, raw data packets and logs. We use the RabbitMQ[2] as the underlying message-passing mechanism. It acts as a secure message broker between all the components through encrypted channels.

Each message contains a routing key and a topic which indicates how to route this message to the relevant input queues of the components. Messages are of

---

[2] https://www.rabbitmq.com/.

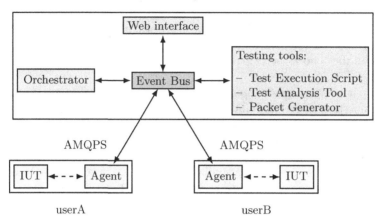

Fig. 2. The F-Interop architecture.

two types: control plane and data plane. Control plane messages relate to the management of an ongoing test session: e.g. start a sniffer, signal the start/end of a test case, etc. Data plane messages contains the raw data exchanged between the IUTs.

Vendors conducts interoperability tests in virtual independent "rooms". We use the virtual host mechanism of RabbitMQ to ensure isolation between concurrent rooms.

This architecture is modular and scalable by design. Components can be added/deleted from the event bus without requiring further coordination. Different components can be run on different (virtual) machines to ensure scalability. Different components can be written in different programming languages.

3.2 Agent: Connecting Users to the Platform

The "agent" is a program a user downloads from the F-Interop website, and which allows him/her to connect an IUT to the F-Interop server. Communication between the agent and the server is authenticated and secure. Through the agent, the F-Interop server can (remotely) interact with the IUT, for example by changing configuration or injecting packets. Similarly, the agent reports events to the server, such as sniffed packets.

3.3 The Orchestrator

The orchestrator plays a purely administrative role: it monitors the users that are connected, activates the rooms currently in use and starts/stops the test sessions. It is also in charge of provisioning the message broker and updating firewall rules when test sessions are activated. It does so by spawning/killing the processes of the different components connected to the event bus. It uses the **supervisor** process control system[3].

3.4   Test Session

A test session can be started once the different users are connected and the necessary components are provisioned by the orchestrator. The role of the test session is to generate verdicts that corresponds to test cases. A test session corresponds to one test description. While the F-Interop platform does not impose a particular organization of a test session (i.e. it operates as a black box which generates test verdicts), it is typically composed of a test execution script, a test analysis tool and (optionally) a packet generator.

Test Execution Script. The test execution script (TExS) is the code that describes the configurations and the steps of each test case. It is a translation of a test case of the test descriptions (TD) into machine understandable language. Just like the TDs, the TExS describes the set of steps that need to be executed. Typically, there are 3 types of steps:

- STIMULI: an action for stimulating the IUT (e.g. sending a CoAP message).
- CHECK: the action of validating the communication (e.g. check that the field X is equal to value Y).
- VERIFY: the action of verifying that an IUT behaves correctly (e.g. verify that resource A updated its value to B).

Test Analysis Tool. The Test Analysis Tool (TAT) is the component that performs the verification of traces during a test session. F-Interop provides TATs for different protocols, which run after the message exchange is finished. The TAT issues three types of verdicts: PASS when test purpose of the test case is verified, FAIL when there is at least one fault, INCONCLUSIVE when the behavior of the IUTs does not apply to the one described in the test purpose. The architecture support TATs which perform step-by-step analysis.

TATs are created both by the F-Interop core team and by external contributors. The F-Interop API specification defines the format of the messages a TAT will receive from the Event Bus, and the format of the messages it can produce.

Packet Generator. In some conformance tests, a packet generator component can be used to generate packets for the IUT. This component can for example implement the behavior of a CoAP server when the IUT implements a CoAP client. Because it has full control over its packet generator, the F-Interop server can purposely generate wrongly formatted messages to verify the correct behavior of the IUT.

---

[3] http://supervisord.org/.

3.5   Web Interface

The F-Interop web interface allows the user to select a test description from a list of available tests, start the execution of the test description and follow the execution of the different test cases. In some cases, the web interface can request the user to take some action (e.g. switch off a node). The web interface also allows the user to retrieve the test report. The web interface communicates with the rest of the system by sending/receiving message over the Event Bus.

4   Example Remote Interoperability Tests

This section shows how the F-Interop architecture is used to execute the CoAP interoperability test from Fig. 2 between userA and userB. userA has implemented a CoAP server, userB a CoAP client. They want to verify that userB's CoAP client can issue a CoAP GET request to userA's CoAP server.

userA and userB agree on a date perform the interoperability testing, and create an account on the F-Interop server. At that date, they download the agent from the F-Interop web site, and connect it to the server using their user credentials. Once connected, the users only interact with the F-Interop web interface.

Fig. 3. Web interface after 7 tests have been run.

On the web interface, they create a common room and select the CoAP test description. Because the CoAP implementations of userA and userB are computer programs, the agent of each user creates a virtual tun interface. The tun interfaces acts as a secure tunnel between userA and userB's agents, which passes through the F-Interop server.

The users then follow the instructions on the web interface: userB issues a CoAP GET request to userA's CoAP server. During this exchange, the F-Interop server captures the packets exchanged. The users then indicate the test is over and verify that the exchange behaved correctly; the F-Interop server analyses the packets exchanged and issues a verdict. Figure 3 shows the web interface.

5 Discussion

F-Interop is an ongoing project. Its architecture is not written in stone and the F-Interop team is always looking to enhance it to be able to handle addition test configurations. This section contains addition features being worked on.

Testbed integration. Several low-power wireless mesh testbeds exist which contain a large number of nodes. The goal of F-Interop is to allow tests to be run on those testbeds, for example by running the user's firmware and a reference firmware side-by-side on different nodes in the testbed. In that context, F-Interop tests could be launched periodically as part of continuous integration.

Accurate end-to-end latency measurement. There is a delay between the user premises and the F-Interop system; in some cases, this delay could code event re-ordering and false verdicts. The F-Interop team is contemplating building a board which the users would use in their premises, and which would synchronize to GPS and timestamp events with a 10–100 ns accuracy.

Energy measurement capabilities at the user. Energy consumption is an important part of any low-power wireless product; some test cases could target energy consumption. A board which would measure the energy consumption of the IUT would enable a large number of addition test cases.

References

1. Bormann, C.: Test Descriptions for ETSI plugtest CoAP#4. Technical report, ETSI, London, United Kingdom, 7–9 March 2014
2. Bormann, C.: 6Lo Test Descriptions, ETSI 6TiSCH/6lo plugtest. Technical report, ETSI, Berlin, Germany, 17–19 July 2016
3. Palattella, M.R., Vilajosana, X., Chang, T., Watteyne, T.: 6TiSCH Interoperability Test Descriptions for the ETSI 6TiSCH/6lo Plugtests. Technical report, ETSI, Berlin, Germany, 17–19 July 2016
4. Shelby, Z., Hartke, K., Bormann, C.: The Constrained Application Protocol (CoAP), June 2014
5. Ziegler, S., Fdida, S., Watteyne, T., Viho, C.: F-Interop - online conformance, interoperability and performance tests for the IoT. In: International Conference on Interoperability in IoT (InterIoT), Paris, France, EAI. Springer, 26–28 October 2016

BMFA: Bi-Directional Multicast Forwarding Algorithm for RPL-based 6LoWPANs

Georgios Z. Papadopoulos[2(✉)], Andreas Georgallides[1], Theo Tryfonas[1], and George Oikonomou[1]

[1] Faculty of Engineering, University of Bristol, Bristol, UK
{a.georgallides,theo.tryfonas,g.oikonomou}@bristol.ac.uk
[2] IRISA, Télécom Bretagne, Institut Mines-Télécom, Rennes, France
georgios.papadopoulos@telecom-bretagne.eu

Abstract. In scenarios involving point-to-multipoint network traffic, transmitting to each destination individually with unicast may lead to poor utilisation of network bandwidth, excessive energy consumption caused by the high number of packets and suffers from low scalability as the number of destinations increases. An alternative approach, would be to use network-layer multicast, where packets are transmitted to multiple destinations simultaneously. In doing so, applications adopting a one-to-many communication paradigm may improve their energy efficiency and bandwidth utilisation. In this paper, we present Bi-directional Multicast Forwarding Algorithm (BMFA), a novel RPL-based multicast forwarding mechanism. BMFA improves its pre-predecessor SMRF in that it allows multicast traffic to travel both upwards as well as downwards in an RPL tree. At the same time, it retains SMRF's low latency and very low energy consumption characteristics. Our performance evaluation results, conducted using the Contiki operating system, show that BMFA outperforms its rival Trickle Multicast/Multicast Protocol for Low power and Lossy Networks (TM/MPL), in terms of reducing both delay and energy consumption.

Keywords: Internet of things · 6LoWPAN · Wireless sensor networks · IPv6 Multicast · Trickle

1 Introduction

In environmental monitoring scenarios, it is expected that networks will be formed by a potentially very high number of sensor nodes and therefore scalability is an essential requirement. In cases when sensor devices are powered by batteries, it is impractical or outright untenable to replace batteries very frequently due to high management cost and possibly hard-to-reach installation locations. Thus, long battery life is important. Low energy consumption may also be considered important in deployments with mains-powered devices, in order to reduce financial cost, but also in order to comply with national and international regulations where applicable.

© ICST Institute for Computer Sciences, Social Informatics and Telecommunications Engineering 2017
N. Mitton et al. (Eds.): InterIoT 2016/SaSeIot 2016, LNICST 190, pp. 18–25, 2017.
DOI: 10.1007/978-3-319-52727-7_3

In scenarios involving point-to-multipoint network traffic, transmitting to each destination individually using unicast at the network layer may lead to poor utilisation of network bandwidth, excessive energy consumption caused by the high number of packets and suffers from low scalability as the number of destinations increases. An alternative approach is to use network-layer multicast, where packets are transmitted to a set of destinations simultaneously. This can lead to energy-efficiency improvements for applications that require one-to-many communications. Examples of such applications include service discovery and network management.

In this paper, we present the design and implementation of a new multicast forwarding algorithm for 6LoWPANs, namely, Bi-Directional Multicast Forwarding Algorithm (BMFA). We demonstrate that BMFA can achieve very low energy consumption and therefore meet the requirements of aforementioned use-cases, ultimately increasing the lifetime of a smart object deployment.

2   Background and Related Work

A number of works in the area of multicast for Internet of Things (IoT) and Wireless Sensor Networks (WSNs) have been proposed. A large number of multicast forwarding solutions encountered in current literature are based on geographic routing, such as those discussed in [1,2]. However, most of those approaches have certain characteristics and make assumptions which render them unsuitable for IPv6-based deployments. For instance, many of them assume that, for every multicast message, the sender is aware of the addresses or unique identifiers of all intended destinations. Additionally, some efforts suffer from poor scalability while others rely on unrealistically large network packets. Finally, they are only applicable where the source as well as all destinations are within the boundaries of the same WSN deployment.

Multicast Protocol for Low-Power and Lossy Networks (MPL) is the standard for multicast forwarding and group management in Low-Power and Lossy Networks (LLNs) [3]. MPL is independent of the protocol used for unicast routing. It will thus operate in Routing Protocol for LLNs (RPL)-based [4] 6LoWPANs, as well as in deployments where RPL is not in use. In a nutshell, MPL routers maintain a cache of multicast datagrams they have seen. Neighbours exchange information about the content of their caches by using ICMPv6 messages. If one node detects that one of its neighbours has not received a multicast datagram that the former has in its cache, it will schedule subsequent forwarding of the datagram(s) in question. The exchange of ICMPv6 messages is governed by trickle [5], thus reducing network control traffic when multicast traffic is not present, but reacting quickly to the arrival of new multicast datagrams.

SMRF [6,7] is a multicast forwarding algorithm based on the topology information provided by RPL. Nodes participating in an RPL network exchange topology information in order to build a Destination Oriented Directed Acyclic Graph (DODAG) and construct their routing tables. When RPL's "Storing with multicast support" Mode of Operation (MOP) is used, a node can join a multicast group by advertising its address in an outgoing Destination Advertisement

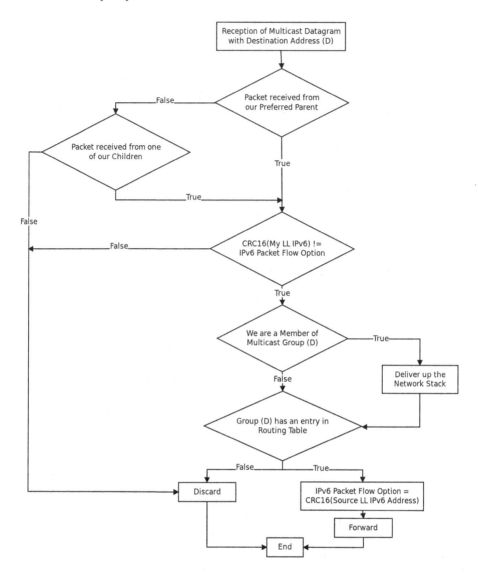

Fig. 1. The BMFA algorithm.

Object (DAO) message. Upon reception of such a message from one of its children, the parent node registers the multicast address in its routing table; then the same address is advertised by the parent in its own DAO messages. When a multicast packet destined to that address arrives, it will be forwarded downwards the tree until it reaches the recipient nodes.

3   BMFA Operation

SMRF is very lightweight but this comes at the cost of a severe limitation: it is only capable of forwarding traffic "downwards" in the RPL DODAG tree [6,7]. In this paper, we present a multicast forwarding algorithm called BFMA, an extended version of SMRF scheme. BFMA's primary design goal is to alleviate this limitation (i.e., allow both upwards and downwards traffic) while at the same time maintaining SMRF's lightweight and energy-efficient nature. In order to support bi-directional traffic and avoid routing loops, BMFA uses the 20 flow-label bits of the IPv6 header. BMFA also uses information provided by RPL's group membership scheme. Its operation is the following (Fig. 1):

- A node will accept an incoming multicast datagram if and only if the digest value in the Flow Label inside the IPv6 header does not contain the digest value of its own Link Local address and if the datagram's link layer source address is the link layer address of either the node's preferred RPL parent or the link layer address of one of its children.
- If the message gets accepted and if the node is member of the multicast group, then the message will get delivered up to the network stack locally.
- If the message gets accepted the packet's Flow Label field is updated to the digest value of the packet sender's link layer source address.
- If the message gets accepted and if there is an entry for the datagram's multicast destination address in the routing table, meaning that a node under us in the RPL structure is a group member, the packet will get forwarded.

4   Performance Evaluation

We have implemented BMFA for the Contiki open-source operating system for the Internet of Things. Contiki also features an implementation of an earlier version of the MPL algorithm, called Trickle Multicast (TM). For this evaluation we therefore compare BMFA with Contiki's implementation of TM, using the Cooja simulator [8]. Our setup consists of 21 simulated nodes, each one of them operating as a multicast traffic source, a group member, or a simple traffic forwarder. Depending on the experiment, all nodes would support either BMFA or TM. Our experiments aim to investigate performance changes of those two algorithms based on different configurations and under different network traffic patterns. Table 1 summarising important simulation parameters.

4.1   Network Delay

We investigate network delay as a factor of traffic bit rate and network density (defined in [7]). As can be observed from Fig. 2, TM does not perform as it was expected based on the configured parameters. For instance, TM configured with Imin = 750 ms leads to the lowest end-to-end delay across the board (for different traffic bit rates per network density). Moreover, end-to-end delay is expected to

Table 1. Simulation setup.

Topology parameters	Value
Topology	$360 \times 200\,\mathrm{m}$
Number of nodes	21 fixed sensors (20 sources)
Node spacing	$x = 6\,\mathrm{m}/y = 8\,\mathrm{m}$
Simulation parameters	Value
Duration	$68\,\mathrm{min}$
Data collection scheme	CBR &VBR
TM	lmin in [125, 500, 700] ms
BMFA	Spread in [2, 4]
Routing model	RPL [4]
Number of hops	Multihop (5 hops maximum)
MAC model	CSMA
Duty cycling	ContikiMAC (CCI 125 ms)
PHY	IEEE 802.15.4
Hardware parameters	Value
Antenna model	Omnidirectional
Radio propagation	$2.4\,\mathrm{GHz}$
Transmission range	TX: 50 m, Interference: 60 m (UDGM)

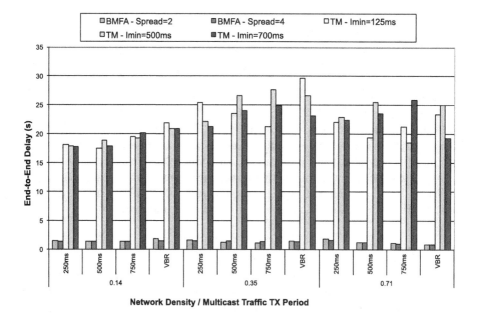

Fig. 2. BMFA vs TM end-to-end delay performance.

be lower as Imin decreases, while our simulation results present the opposite. Lastly, high delays were anticipated under TM since it uses link layer broadcasts, which are fundamentally inefficient under ContikiMAC, as demonstrated in [7].

On the other hand, when using BMFA in low-density topologies (i.e., up to 0.35), the end-to-end delay declines slightly as the inter-packet delay increases, while when the bit rate decreases (Variable Bit Rate with 1–2 s inter-packet delay) overall delay reaches its maximum. This is caused by packets spending more time in a node's cache when the bit rate increases; packets do not get transmitted until all packets preceding them are forwarded first. Furthermore, an inter-packet delay of more than 1 s leads to the opposite results, since all cached packets get forwarded before the next one arrives. On the other hand, for high densities (i.e., 0.71) the delay continues its descending trend as the inter-packet delay increases. Based on the fact that for high network densities a node is expected to be selected as preferred parent from a greater number of nodes (RPL's DODAG becomes shallow and wide), more packets are expected to wait into its cache until they get forwarded; in this case packets transmitted with VBR arrive neither too soon nor too late to the recipient nodes, resulting to even better results. To summarize the performance of the two algorithms, BMFA outperforms TM by at least five times under most configurations.

4.2   Energy Consumption

Through the facilities provided by Contiki's energy consumption estimation module, (Energest [9]), we measured the time each node spent in different

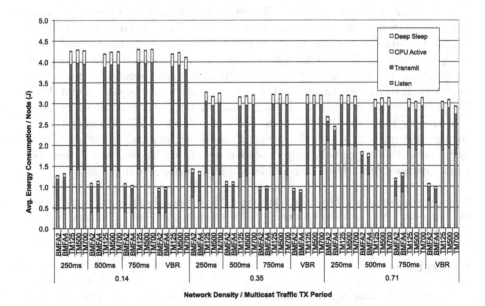

Fig. 3. BMFA vs TM average node energy consumptions.

power consumption states (MCU active; RF listening/receiving, RF transmitting). Since we are simulating Texas Instruments MSP430F5438 experimenter board nodes, we converted these time values to estimated energy consumption based on typical datasheet power consumption levels at an operating voltage of 3.0 V.

For TM it can be observed (Fig. 3) that under higher network densities, less energy is consumed due to the fact that agreement between all nodes can be achieved with fewer ICMPv6 control message exchanges. This can be also observed by the fact that as density increases, less energy is required for transmitting than for listening. For BMFA, irrespective of network density, as the inter-packet delay between the transmitted packets increases, overall energy consumption decreases since fewer packets are forwarded. In the case of a very dense network (0.71) and for high bit rates, we can see that energy consumption with BMFA approaches the one observed with TM. This happens because nodes are consuming too much energy by keeping the radio on as a result of picking up transmissions from their large number of neighbours, despite the fact that they only forward packets received only from their children or preferred parent. By comparing the two algorithms we can see that BMFA is more energy efficient than TM since it forwards each packet only once and there is no additional ICMPv6 control message exchange. Moreover, we must highlight that the energy consumption attributed to CPU activity indicates TM's higher algorithmic complexity.

5   Conclusion

In this paper, we have presented BMFA, a multicast forwarding mechanism that minimises network-wide energy consumption. We have implemented BMFA for the Contiki OS and have undertaken a thorough performance evaluation using the Cooja simulator. Our results show a typical trade-off between network performance, energy consumption and reliability. More specifically, our results show that BMFA outperforms TM, in terms of reducing the end-to-end delay, design complexity, code size and energy consumption, while on the other hand, TM severely outperforms BMFA in terms of reliability. Finally, note that as documented in [6,7], the performance of multicast forwarding for all engines discussed in this paper is heavily dependent on the underlying MAC layer. For a more detailed description of possible optimizations see [6,7].

Acknowledgements. The research leading to these results has received funding from the European Union's Seventh Framework Programme (FP7/2007-2013) under grant agreement no.609094.

References

1. Carzaniga, A., Khazaei, K., Kuhn, F.: Oblivious low-congestion multicast routing in wireless networks. In: Proceedings of the 13th ACM International Symposium on Mobile Ad Hoc Networking and Computing (MobiHoc), pp. 155–164(2012)

2. Feng, C.H., Zhang, I.D.Y., Heinzelman, W.B.: Stateless multicast protocol for Ad Hoc networks. IEEE Trans. Mob. Comput. **11**(2), 240–253 (2012)
3. Hui, J., Kelsey, R.: Multicast Protocol for Low-Power and Lossy Networks (MPL), RFC 7731, February 2016
4. Winter, T., Thubert, P., Brandt, A., Hui, J., Kelsey, R., Levis, P., Pister, K., Struik, R., Vasseur, J.A.R.: RPL: IPv6 Routing Protocol for Low-Power and Lossy Networks, RFC 6550 (2012)
5. Levis, P., Clausen, T., Hui, J., Gnawali, O., Ko, J.: The Trickle Algorithm, RFC 6206, March 2011
6. Oikonomou, G., Philips, I.: Stateless multicast forwarding with RPL in 6LoWPAN sensor networks. In: Proceedings of the IEEE International Conference on Pervasive Computing and Communications Workshops (PERCOM Workshops), pp. 272–277 (2012)
7. Oikonomou, G., Philips, I., Tryfonas, T.: IPv6 multicast forwarding in RPL-based wireless sensor networks. Wirel. Pers. Commun. **73**(3), 1089–1116 (2013)
8. Österlind, F., Dunkels, A., Eriksson, J., Finne, N., Voigt, T.: Cross-level sensor network simulation with COOJA. In: Proceedings of the 31st Annual IEEE International Conference on Local Computer Networks (LCN) (2006)
9. Dunkels, A., Osterlind, F., Tsiftes, N., He, Z.: Software-based On-line energy estimation for sensor nodes. In: Proceedings of the 4th ACN Workshop on Embedded Networked Sensors (EmNets), pp. 28–32 (2007)

Synchronization Abstractions and Separation of Concerns as Key Aspects to the Interoperability in IoT

Marcio Ferreira Moreno[1](✉), Renato Cerqueira[1], and Sérgio Colcher[2]

[1] IBM Research, Av. Pasteur, 138 and 146 – Botafogo,
Rio de Janeiro (RJ), Brazil
{mmoreno,rcerq}@br.ibm.com
[2] Department of Informatics – PUC-Rio, Rua Marques de São Vicente,
225 – Gávea, Rio de Janeiro (RJ) 22451-900, Brazil
colcher@inf.puc-rio.br

Abstract. In this paper we argue that synchronization abstractions could be used as the glue that tie together the interactions between 'things' in an IoT environment. We also support that this is analog to what is used in distributed multimedia applications. Using this argument, we propose in this paper that IoT solutions, protocols and applications should benefit from standardized multimedia tools like specification languages and corresponding middleware support platforms as a means for harmonization and interoperability. Additionally, we extend our recent contributions in favor of a separation of concerns in multimedia systems, in which synchronization support can operate independently of other features. More specifically, the main contribution of this paper is the discussions about how media synchronization challenges can enroll the Internet of Things research area, where distributed sensors and actuators are specified as media objects and can be related to usual hypermedia objects, all synchronized in time and space, in what we call the "Synchronism of Things".

Keywords: Internet of Things · Synchronism of things · Interoperability · Ginga · NCL

1 Introduction

IoT has emerged as a promise for a completely new ecosystem made for the interconnection of "things" that will open the doors for emerging and compelling applications like smart cities, smart grids, health and fitness wearable devices and agro-business sensor powered equipment that could revolutionize productivity. IoT can be thought as representing a new wave on Internet evolution technologies, that brings not only Machine-to-Machine (M2M) communications to the world of interconnected people and business processes, but also inspires new thoughts over the meaning of what is interconnection itself.

To reach the full potential of the IoT, however, it is not sufficient for things to just be connected to the Internet; they also need to be found, accessed, managed and potentially connected to other things. To enable this interaction, a degree of

© ICST Institute for Computer Sciences, Social Informatics and Telecommunications Engineering 2017
N. Mitton et al. (Eds.): InterIoT 2016/SaSeIot 2016, LNICST 190, pp. 26–32, 2017.
DOI: 10.1007/978-3-319-52727-7_4

interoperability is necessary that goes beyond simple protocol interoperability as provided by the Internet [1].

Standard organizations and community forums have been working towards reference models, architectures and specific standards for different parts or levels within those models in order to bring some structure to the chaos, trying to lessen the gap between the different vertical domains and help industry not to jump into proprietary solutions. From the network point of view, protocol interoperability is the main focus, and organizations like IEEE and ITU-T have been working very hard trying to overcome the challenges of bringing together efficient protocols like the various low power networking protocols (ZigBee, ZWave, and Bluetooth), traditional networking protocols (Ethernet, WiFi) and new technologies (5G) [2]. The IETF community has also been involved in foundational IoT technologies such as IPv6 and the Constrained Application Protocol (CoAP) focusing on getting constrained devices and sensor networks connected to the Internet [3].

But, as Blackstock and Lea state [3], before addressing interoperability, there must be some agreement on what interoperability means, and about the degree of interoperability required, as well as on its implications for IoT system and application developers.

Actually, we could think that application level interoperability is also desirable. In fact, the Internet of Things Architecture project (IoT-A) is proposing an architectural reference model for IoT interoperability, along with key components that deals with application level issues like search, discovery, and interaction between things [3]. But there is also a multiplicity of competing application level protocols such as CoAP (Constrained Application Protocol), MQTT (Message Queue Telemetry Transport) and XMPP (Extensible Messaging and Presence Protocol) that have been proposed by various organizations to become the *de facto* standard to provide communication interoperability, each of which with unique characteristics that happens to be adequate for different types of IoT applications. However, as pointed out by Desai et al. [2], a scalable IoT architecture should be independent of messaging protocol standards, while also providing integration and translation between various popular messaging protocols. Moreover, while exchanging information by messages in an efficient way is an important requirement at this level of abstraction, the synchronization that should be obtained when things are engaged in these communication processes seems to be left aside.

In this paper we argue that synchronization abstractions should be treated as the glue that tie together all the interactions between things. We also support that this is not much different than what is used in distributed multimedia applications. Using this argument, we propose that IoT applications should benefit from standardized multimedia tools like specification languages and corresponding middleware support platforms as a means for acquiring interoperability.

The key issue in a multimedia system is the support for temporal and spatial synchronization among media assets, in its broad sense. In this work, we extend our recent contributions in favor of a separation of concerns in multimedia systems, in which synchronization support can operate independently of other features. More specifically, the main contribution of this paper is the discussions about how media synchronization challenges can enroll the Internet of Things research area, where distributed sensors and actuators are specified as media objects and can be related to usual hypermedia objects, all synchronized in time and space, in what we call the "Synchronism of Things" (SoT).

2 Separation of Concerns: Isolating the Synchronization Support

The evolution of multimedia applications has continuously created new challenges for systems that support media synchronization. Besides the development of new communication technologies and the advances in computational resources, high-quality media objects and new compression techniques led to novel requirements for media synchronization. Multi-sensorial media (mulsemedia) presentations has also introduced different requirements [4], where media objects that state traditional visual content types (i.e. text, images, and video) can be related with media objects that target other human senses (e.g. olfactics, haptics etc.).

As introduced in Sect. 1, in the SoT perspective, the new requirements go beyond the use of multi-sensorial media to enhance user Quality of Experience, as usual in mulsemedia. Indeed, the idea is to introduce how media synchronization challenges enrolls the Internet of Things research area, where different distributed sensors and actuators are specified as media objects and related to usual objects, all synchronized in time and space.

The separation of concerns in this paper extrapolates our recent contributions [5–7], arguing in favor of architectures of multimedia systems being divided in two modules at least: one to support the synchronization of media assets, controlling the logic of the execution; other in charge of transporting and handling the backend mechanisms of media assets. In this paper, the former is called Execution Manager and the latter Multithing Backend.

In the separation of concerns, the Execution Manager can operate independently of the underlying backend features, making it possible for developers or end-users to add and update features (for instance, having new logics for sensors or actuators added as plug-ins) dynamically without needing to make changes to the host Manager (host). Open application programming interface allows third parties to create plug-ins that interact with the host application. A stable plug-in API allows both third-party plug-ins to continue functioning as the original version changes and to increase the lifetime of obsolete applications.

These concepts are essential for coexistence and interoperability of different IoT solutions and protocols, and were applied in our previous work. More specifically, in the specification language named NCL and in its middleware Ginga [7]. Indeed, NCL has a strict separation between application content and application structure. NCL does not define any media itself. Instead, it defines the glue that relates media objects in time and space. NCL documents (NCL application specifications) only refer to media content. Any media object has a set of properties and some content. Content can be the logic of sensor/actuator, samples of video, audio, images and text, or any code chunk in some specification language. Properties are usually related to the content, like the positioning of a mechanical arm, the format of data being sensed, and others.

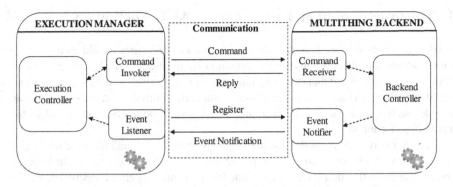

Fig. 1. Separation of concerns in multimedia synchronism support.

Figure 1 illustrates the proposed separation of concerns. The Execution Manager is responsible for reading the document specification and for building an execution plan, using a sub-module named Execution Controller. The Multithing Backend transport, decodes, processes, and handles media content, using a sub-module called Backend Controller.

Nevertheless, this separation of concerns goes beyond modularization. Those two main modules are deeply separated from each other, by means of process isolation. For this reason, they also include sub-modules that provide inter-process communication. The Execution Manager defines the Command Invoker and the Event Listener. The Multithing Backend defines the Command Receiver and the Event Notifier.

The modules communicate either (i) to handle the execution of commands or (ii) to handle the occurrence of events (e.g. temporal events, user-generated events). The design of the first type of communication resembles the Distributed Command design pattern, while the second type resembles the Distributed Observer design pattern [5, 8].

The Command Invoker submodule is responsible for sending commands to the Multithing Backend. These commands can either request the execution of an action or query the value of a variable (that is, a media object or system property).

The Multithing Backend receives commands through the Command Receiver. This submodule parses the requests to check whether they are valid and forwards them to the Backend Controller. The Command Receiver may send a reply message, notifying whether the Multithing Backend was able to meet the request or not.

The Event Listener is responsible for receiving event notifications. First, it registers itself as a listener (observer) to be notified of events during the presentation. Upon receiving an event notification, this submodule converts the notification into the data structure expected by the Presentation Controller and delivers the event.

Finally, the Event Notifier is in charge of notifying the registered observers about events. The event types notified depend on the implementation. To reduce the message traffic, this module can implement a filtering approach, in which the observers inform upon registration the types of events they can handle. The Event Notifier would then send notifications only when there is a match between the event type and the filters of an observer.

3   The Synchronism of Things with an NCL Application

In NCL every <media> element can have <area> and <property> child elements. An <area> element defines a subset of information units of some media-object content. Thus, an <area> element can define an interval of time, a subset of data in a sensor or a text string. Since media objects can also contain code chunks, an <area> element can also delineate a code chunk; for example, a function of the application, coded in the media object content.

The <property> element defines the name attribute, which indicates the name of a property or of a property group of its parent media object, and the value attribute, an optional attribute that defines an initial value for the name property. Property can define where and how content resulting from the media object processing is executed or presented. In media objects with imperative code content, the <property> element can also refer to a specific code chunk through its name attribute, in which case the value attribute has input parameters to be passed to the code chunk.

Figure 2 depicts a very simple NCL application illustrating how media objects encapsulate concepts of new media types and how the NCL execution engine is in charge of orchestrate the execution of documents with these different media assets that can be of different IoT standards and protocols. NCL defines the <ncl> root element and its child <head> and <body> elements, following the terminology adopted by W3C standards to structure documents. The <body> element includes <port>, <media>, and <link> child elements. The <port> elements externalize interfaces of child media-objects of a composition (the <body> element in this case). When an NCL application is started without specifying a <port>, the execution of every media object associated to every <port> element is started. There are three <media> elements in the example. All of them use remote node.js[1] entry points to communicate with remote content, which must be processed by a plug-in whose location is www.ginga.ncl.org.br/plugins. The plug-in use the IoT communication infrastructure of IBM (e.g. IoT Foundation, Watson IoT Platform, and REST & Real-time APIs)[2] to exchange data between sensors and actuators. Finally, three <link> elements establish spatial and temporal relationships among the media objects.

The Execution Manager of Ginga starts the application with the presentation of the NCL object "oil": a player that uses a sensor designed to extract oil parameters during a distillation process. If the sensor detects the end of the process, the player notifies the end of the "oil" component execution to its parent controller (the Execution Manager of Ginga). At this moment, the condition of <link id = "l2"> is satisfied, starting the "highlight" object. The player of this object is a cognitive computing system designed to extract and register the highlights of the distillation process.

During the "oil" object presentation, if the sensor detects changes in the "viscosity" parameter, the node.js player (plug-in) notifies the parent Execution Manager the start-attribution-event occurrence. As a consequence, the condition of the <link id = "l1"> is satisfied, setting the "visbreaker" property of the "distillation" media

---

[1] https://nodejs.org/.

[2] https://internetofthings.ibmcloud.com.

```xml
<?xml version="1.0" encoding="UTF-8"?>
<nclid="SoT" xmlns="http://www.ncl.org.br/NCL3.0/EDTVProfile">

  <head>
  ...
  </head>

  <body>
<portid="entryPoint" component="oil"/>

    <mediaid="oil"src="nodejs/oilsensor" descriptor="oDesc"
player="www.ginga.ncl.org.br/plugins">
<propertyvalue="viscosity"/>
</media>

    <mediaid="highlights"src="nodejs/highlights" descriptor="hDesc"
player="www.ginga.ncl.org.br/plugins"/>

    <mediaid="distillation"src="nodejs/oilactuator" descriptor="dDesc"
player="www.ginga.ncl.org.br/plugins">
<propertyname="visbreaker"/>
</media>

    <linkid="l1"xconnector="onEndAttributionSet">
<bindrole="onEndAttribution" component="oil" interface="viscosity"/>
<bindrole="set" component="distillation" interface="visbreaker"/>
<bindParamname="var" value="$getValue"/>
</bind>
<bindrole="getValue" component="oil" interface="viscosity"/>
</link>

    <linkid="l2"xconnector="onEndStart">
<bindrole="onEnd component="oil"/>
<bindrole="start" component="highlights"/>
</link>

  </body>
</ncl>
```

Fig. 2. NCL example: a domain-specific language with synchronization abstractions to promote interoperability between IoT sensors and actuators.

object to the current value of "viscosity". When the "distillation" plug-in receives the "viscosity" value, it executes the node.js code, the "visbreaker" method, passing the value as a parameter. As a consequence, the actuator coupled with the "distillation" player executes the corresponding operation.

4   Final Remarks and Future Directions

Standard organizations and community forums have been working towards reference models, architectures and specific standards for different parts or levels within those models in order to bring some structure to the chaos, trying to lessen the gap between the different vertical domains and help industry not to jump into proprietary solutions. The main contribution of this paper is to present synchronization abstractions in form of a specification language and the separation of concerns to isolate key-issues in architectures as a solution to the coexistence and interoperability challenge in IoT. The separation of concerns combined with the definition of an API for plug-ins allows the system evolution without the need of modifying its synchronization support. More important, the model specifies calls that enables handling synchronization issues. Among other benefits, Ginga plug-in API enables the presentation of new types of media, allowing for applications that can synchronize sensors, actuators, and the usual media objects, in time and space. The drawback of this approach is to have all IoT mechanisms centralized in the plug-ins. To address this issue, we intent to study how NCL and Ginga functionalities are related to the ones present in Node-RED[3]. Node-RED is an authoring tool to specify data flows relating IoT devices, APIs and online services. Another future direction we aim to pursue is the use of knowledge engineering and cognitive computing agents in the description of NCL applications. We argue that this could bring the description of NCL-IoT applications to another level, allowing, for instance, the use of semantics on sensors and actuators as well as the use of cognitive computing analysis over sensed data. Our recent works [9–11] consist in a first step in this direction.

References

1. Blackstock, M., Lea, R.: IoT interoperability: a hub-based approach. In: 2014 International Conference on the Internet of Things (IoT), Cambridge, MA, USA, pp. 79–84. doi:10.1109/IOT.2014.7030119
2. Desai, P., Sheth, A., Anantharam, P.: Semantic gateway as a service architecture for IoT interoperability. In: 2015 IEEE International Conference on Mobile Services (MS), New York City, NY, USA, pp. 313–319. doi:10.1109/MobServ.2015.51
3. Blackstock, M., Lea, R.: Toward interoperability in a web of things. In: Mattern, F., Santini, S., Canny, J.F., Langheinrich, M., Rekimoto, J. (eds.) The 2013 ACM Conference, Zurich, Switzerland, pp. 1565–1574. doi:10.1145/2494091.2497591
4. Yuan, Z., Bi, T., Muntean, G.-M., Ghinea, G.: Perceived synchronization of mulsemedia services. IEEE Trans. Multimed. **17**(7), 957–966 (2015)
5. Moreno, M.F., Santos, R., Lima, G., Soares, L.F.G.: Deepening the separation of concerns in the implementation of multimedia systems. In: ACM SAC (2016)
6. Soares, L.F.G., Moreno, M.F., Marinho, R.S.: Ginga-NCL architecture for plug-ins. Softw. Pract. Exp. **43**(4), 449–463 (2013). doi:10.1002/spe.2144
7. Moreno, M.F., Soares, L., Cerqueira, R.: A component-based architecture for Ginga. In: 13th International Conference on Software Engineering Research and Practice, pp. 76–82
8. Soares, L.F.G.S., Moreno, M.F., Guedes, A.L.V.: Controlling the focus and input events in multimedia applications. In: ACM SAC 2015, Salamanca, Spain, 13–17 April 2015
9. Moreno, M.F., Brandao, R.R.M., Cerqueira, R.: Extending hypermedia conceptual models to support hyperknowledge specifications. In: IEEE ISM, San Jose, CA, USA (2016, in press)
10. Moreno, M.F., Brandao, R.R.M., Cerqueira, R.: Towards a conceptual model for cognitive-intensive practices. In: IEEE ISM, San Jose, CA, USA (2016, in press)
11. Moreno, M.F., Brandao, R.R.M., Cerqueira, R.: NCM 3.1: a conceptual model for hyperknowledge document engineering. In: ACM DocEng, Vienna, Austria (2016)

---

[3] http://nodered.org/.

Providing Interoperability for Autonomic Control of Connected Devices

François Aïssaoui[1], Guillaume Garzone[1(✉)], and Nicolas Seydoux[1,2]

[1] LAAS-CNRS, Univ. de Toulouse, INSA, UT Capitole, Toulouse, France
{francois.aissaoui,guillaume.garzone,nicolas.seydoux}@laas.fr
[2] IRIT, Maison de la Recherche, Univ. Toulouse Jean Jaurès, Toulouse, France

Abstract. In the IoT, data is exchanged and used by heterogeneous devices in machine-to-machine communications. Managing complex systems is at the core of autonomic computing and a key topic in the IoT. Therefore, interoperability is a central issue, at both the syntactic and the semantic level. To tackle syntactic and architectural interoperability, standards allow systems to connect and exchange structured data. However, for data to be used, semantic interoperability must be ensured to provide meaning and consistency. In this paper we provide syntactic and semantic interoperability solutions in a home automation autonomic system.

Keywords: Syntactic interoperability · Semantic interoperability · Standards · OM2M · Open-source · oneM2M

1 Interoperability in Complex System Management

The Internet of Things (IoT) is a technological paradigm that brings tremendous changes in domains as various as agriculture, smart cities, home automation, manufacturing, transportation, energy management, health, etc. [1].

However, the silo-oriented design of solutions leads to an important vertical fracturing, raising a need for openness. Indeed, this fracturing is a cause of interoperability issues, a major concern for the development of the IoT, motivating standard organizations and open source communities to address these obstacles.

Furthermore, the lack of interoperability brings scalability issues: connecting devices or applications that are not interoperable requires the development of a dedicated middleware, which is a time-consuming process that has to be renewed each time new components are integrated. Hence, the system management becomes complex, and a way to automate it is using the autonomic computing paradigm [2], introduced in [3]. An autonomic system is the association of a managed entity and an autonomic agent in charge of controlling it, allowing the system administrator to only give high-level policy to the agent who will enforce them on the underlying entity. The issue in the deployment of such a system is to ensure interoperability between the manager and the managed entities, both at a syntactical and at a semantic level.

© ICST Institute for Computer Sciences, Social Informatics and Telecommunications Engineering 2017
N. Mitton et al. (Eds.): InterIoT 2016/SaSeIot 2016, LNICST 190, pp. 33–40, 2017.
DOI: 10.1007/978-3-319-52727-7_5

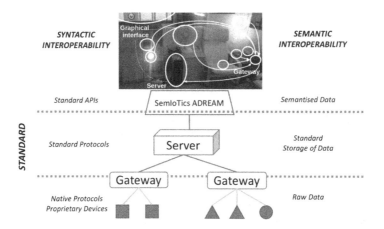

Fig. 1. Overview of the system: devices network and autonomic controler

In this paper, we will focus on a home automation use case with an instrumented apartment inside a connected building, combined with an automation solution that ensures monitoring and control of the place. An overview of this system is shown on Fig. 1. In this context, two main issues are at stake: **syntactic interoperability** to interact with heterogeneous devices, and **semantic interoperability** to provide meaningful and machine-understandable data.

The remaining of this paper is structured as follows: first, the role of interoperability in autonomic solutions for the IoT is studied. Then, our contribution is described in two parts: OM2M, an open-source implementation of the oneM2M standard, is presented as a syntactic interoperability provider, and SemIoTics, a software based on a semantic knowledge base, is presented as a semantic interoperability provider. As an illustration, we provide the real experimentation setting we used before concluding this paper.

2   Autonomic Computing and Interoperability for the IoT

A complete autonomic agent requires both syntactic and semantic interoperability to be fully functional in order to manage a set of connected devices. We chose to implement the MAPE-K loop, an autonomic control structure presented in [3]. An instance of this loop in an IoT context is discussed in [4].

The loop is structured in four phases: *Monitoring*, *Analysis*, *Planning*, and *Execution*, that we implemented in our use case. Monitoring and Execution are the two phases where the autonomic agent is in direct contact with the monitored system. In the **Monitoring** phase, raw sensor data is collected by the system. In the **Execution** phase, commands are sent to the actuators (the devices having an impact on the physical world, e.g. lamps or heating systems). These two phases require syntactic interoperability that ensures the communication between the autonomic agent and the heterogeneous set of devices. Analysis and Planning are two more abstract phases where the agent implements high level policies. **Analysis** is the abstraction of the collected data into meaningful symptoms. **Planning** is the decision-making process where the system determines the actions to be performed through actionable nodes. These two phases are enhanced by semantic interoperability that eases contextualization and reasoning on data. Some existing work such as [5] propose both syntactic and semantic interoperability solutions, but are not based on standards, and not dedicated to autonomic computing. Most of the existing work is either dedicated to one type interoperability or the other, that is why the rest of this section will be dedicated to the study of these contributions separately.

For Monitoring and Execution, syntactic interoperability: In high-tech domains, horizontal syntactical interoperability is often achieved by the usage of standards for data formats, architectures, interfaces, or even exchange protocols. Many standards are dedicated to the IoT, that can be classified in three categories:

- *Solutions based on Standard Definition Organizations (SDO),* such as ETSI, KETI, TIA... Multiple SDO came together with more than 200 companies to create **oneM2M**[1]. It is a consortium providing a global and high level functional architecture based on a REST architecture. The **OSGi alliance**[2] and the **Open Mobile Alliance**[3] are similar open standard organizations. The OSGi alliance provides an abstraction layer based on the OSGi framework to represent a set of heterogeneous devices, and the OMA develops standards in the telecommunication industry.
- *Solutions proposed by industrial consortiums,* such as **OIC**[4], **AllJoyn**[5] or the Broadband forum[6].
- *Other alliances or partnerships* exist, supported by leader companies such as Google in the case of **Thread**[7] or Apple for the **Apple Homekit**[8]

Furthermore, different protocols contribute to the ecosystem such as LWM2M, a device management protocol based on CoAP, a lightweight equivalent of HTTP [6] or MQTT[9], a publish-subscribe protocol. In this paper, we focus on oneM2M since it provides syntactic interoperability but also aims to bring semantic interoperability features [7] necessary for the autonomic control.

For Analysis and Planning, semantic interoperability: The data manipulated by the autonomic agent comes from heterogeneous sources, and can be

---

[1] http://www.onem2m.org/.
[2] https://www.osgi.org/.
[3] http://openmobilealliance.org/.
[4] http://openconnectivity.org.
[5] https://allseenalliance.org.
[6] https://www.broadband-forum.org/.
[7] http://threadgroup.org/.
[8] https://developer.apple.com/homekit/.
[9] http://docs.oasis-open.org/mqtt/mqtt/v3.1.1/os/mqtt-v3.1.1-os.html.

expressed in different formats. Existing work such as [8] tackles this problem by proposing enrichment techniques to transform raw data into knowledge conform to the W3C recommendations. Once enriched, collected data becomes exploitable and can be abstracted into higher-level knowledge as in [9], which is useful in our case of symptom computing in the MAPE-K loop. The knowledge base of an autonomic agent can be expressed in different formalisms [2], in particular using ontologies and semantic web technologies, which provide a meaningful unambiguous knowledge representation.

3   Eclipse OM2M: A Standard and Open Source Platform

Spreading the IoT through openness and open source: Considering the actual ecosystem, openness is an important criteria in the success of the projects to come: developing one's own entire solution is complicated, time consuming and not always relevant. To address this important issue, different entities contribute to break the vertical fragmentation and offer alternative solutions as standard organizations, but also open source communities.

As an example, the Eclipse foundation hosts several open source projects providing implementations of solutions, standards, services, frameworks, protocols, etc. that enable an open IoT[10]. The cooperation between standards and open source is particularly interesting since it ensures a better feedback from the developers community and a wider spread usage of interoperable solutions.

OM2M a middleware for syntactic interoperability: Since 2013 the LAAS develops a horizontal standard platform: OM2M[11]. The project started being an implementation of the European SmartM2M ETSI Standard [10] and now implements the oneM2M standard since November 2015 thanks to our contribution. OM2M is an open source project hosted by the Eclipse foundation, and is part of the Eclipse IoT working group.

OM2M is a horizontal service platform for IoT interoperability providing a RESTful Application Programming Interface (API) with a generic set of service capabilities. Its architecture is based on the OSGI framework, and is extensible via a plugin system. The aim of this kind of platform is to enable the development of services independently of the underlying heterogeneous network of devices. It facilitates the deployment of IoT applications by creating a standard abstraction of Things so that applications can be developed independently of the devices or the platforms. OM2M can be used on different levels in an IoT architecture: at the top level, that is to say on the server level, or on intermediary nodes of the topology, or even on the lower nodes directly connected to the objects. Moreover, implementing the standard makes OM2M interoperable with other implementations of oneM2M and has been tested during several plug-tests.

In a nutshell, OM2M provides an interoperability layer regarding the architecture and protocols, thanks to the oneM2M standard specifications. The platform can be executed at different levels in an IoT topology, and is extensible.

---

[10] http://iot.eclipse.org/.
[11] http://om2m.org/.

At this point, a sufficient level of abstraction is reached and we can focus on data formalism issues and semantic interoperability. In our case, OM2M is deployed on the gateways and the server (cf. Fig. 1) to connect devices to the system and expose them in a standard representation.

4 Toward Semantic Interoperability

4.1 Why Syntactic Interoperability Is Not Sufficient

Semantic interoperability is achieved when interacting systems attribute the same meaning to the content of their exchanges. It requires systems to communicate and to be able to parse the received data: it cannot be built without syntactic interoperability. On the other hand, two systems syntactically interoperable can have semantic discrepancies: for instance, they can exchange sensor observations in XML, but one may format the timestamp MM-DD-YYYY, while the other may use a DD-MM-YYYY format. The two systems will be able to parse the data of each other, but will wrongfully attribute the same meaning to it. This very simple case can be extended to all classic structured data models: relational databases, XML, JSON, etc.

In that case, the first solution to achieve semantic interoperability is a one-by-one model mapping. However, this approach is not scalable in complex systems, where several different data models can dynamically interact, which is the case in many IoT architectures. Another more suitable approach is to use shared data models rich enough to be used unambiguously, such as ontologies. Their level of formalism makes them meaningful for the software agents, helping to bridge the gap between different syntactic data models. Data models can be annotated to be aligned with ontologies, and raw data can be enriched to become semantically enabled. The association of an ontology and the data it describes is called a knowledge base.

4.2 A Knowledge Base Centric Autonomic Agent

In a connected devices network, many nodes only have limited data models (mostly raw values or simple API calls), when higher-level applications have a much more complex data representation (value, unit, originating/destination device, device reliability, location, etc.). Ensuring end-to-end data consistency is among the challenges listed in [11], and it is one of the goals of semantic interoperability. SemioTics is an autonomic application built on top of OM2M (cf. Fig. 1), featuring a knowledge base as its core component: it is used at every step of the MAPE-K loop, and it holds the high-level policies defined by the system administrators. SemioTics extends the notion of end-to-end consistency: the data from the system is not only enriched so that its meaning is maintained, but new knowledge is derived from it, and reinjected into the managed entity.

The raw measures generated by the sensors are enriched by SemioTics using ontologies as SSN[12] for sensor and observations, or IoT-O[13] for IoT-related

---

[12] https://www.w3.org/2005/Incubator/ssn/ssnx/ssn.

[13] https://www.irit.fr/recherches/MELODI/ontologies/IoT-O.

knowledge: actuator and actuation, device and service, etc. Being described with meaningful vocabularies, the observations generated by the system as well as the knowledge regarding the system itself become semantically interoperable (*Semantised data* on Fig. 1). This knowledge can be manipulated by the system administrator to express high-level policies, or can be exchanged with remote systems. Finally, the agents converts inferred meaningful knowledge back into low-level data to control the devices: semantic interoperability is brought seamlessy to the devices unaware of semantic models.

Standards also have a role to play in the domain of semantic interoperability: for instance, the oneM2M standard proposes its own ontology[14] to describe concepts related to its architecture and to IoT in general. Two ontologies aligned with the same reference ontology become semantically interoperable, so the emergence of standard ontologies and the reuse of existing resources are key elements to semantic interoperability. The integration of a knowledge base in the autonomic agent allows to integrate evolving external knowledge, and to ensure semantic consistency from the monitoring to the execution.

5   Use Case and Experimental Setting

SemIoTics is deployed on top of *OM2M* for the autonomic control of an apartment, which includes a connected devices architecture with real-world constraints. The experimentation flat is located in the ADREAM building[15], and the autonomic agent is a software that ensures that user preferences about the environment (temperature, luminosity) are respected (cf. top of Fig. 1). The connected devices (both sensors and actuators) come from different brands, and they are based on heterogeneous technologies, connected to two different gateways. These gateways are connected to a server where the autonomic agent is running. This agent is twofold: it includes a horizontal integration layer to communicate seamlessly with the devices, and a control plane using semantic technologies to make decisions. For the lower-level nodes (around 10), different technologies are featured:

- Phidgets for temperature, luminosity and humidity sensor, legacy lamp and fan controlled via a smart plug
- EnOcean for a battery-less remote
- Philips HUE lamps
- ZigBee to control the heater

These lower-level nodes are connected to two different gateways, a Beagle-Bone Black and an Intel Edison, both running an instance of the OM2M platform. They gather the data and provide a standardized RESTful interface to access the devices. At the core of the network, a server runs an instance of the OM2M server side. The gateways are registered on the server, which provides a

---

[14] http://www.onem2m.org/technical/onem2m-ontologies.
[15] https://www.laas.fr/public/en/adream.

Table 1. Step-by-step use case

Use case phase	Interoperability type at stake	Details
Monitoring	Syntactic	Collection of the sensor raw observations by OM2M
	Semantic	From raw measure to RDF representation: "ambiant air is 25.5 °C in the living room"
Analysis	Semantic	Using user preference, infer symptom: "The living room is too hot"
Planning	Semantic	Using logical reasoning and high-level policies, infer action: "Set AC to 23 °C in living room"
Execution	Semantic	Translation of the high-level action to an actual actuation command
	Syntactic	Execution of the call on the actuator by OM2M

common interface for the whole system. SemIoTics accesses devices through the server, discovering resources and subscribing to the sensors matching its needs (Table 1).

6 Conclusion and Future Work

This paper focuses on interoperability issues in autonomic systems and IoT considering standards and provides an open source implementation. Through a home automation use case, we highlighted on two types of interoperability: *syntactic* and *semantic*. The role of standards (as syntactic interoperability providers) is shown with the description of OM2M, an open-source implementation of the oneM2M standard. Then, SemIoTics is introduced to show the role of semantic interoperability at each step of the autonomic system based on MAPE-K loop.

From now, standards are developing toward the integration of both syntactic and semantic interoperability (as in oneM2M or in the W3C WoT IG[16]), which comforts our approach. Future works will focus on the scalability of our approach, in order to adapt it to a whole smart building and even to a smart city deployment.

Acknowledgements. This work has been cofunded by a "Chaire d'Attractivitè"? of the IDEX Program of the Universitè Fèderale de Toulouse Midi-Pyrènèes, Grant 2014-345 and a FEDER-FSE 2014-2020 found of the Règion Midi-Pyrènèes and the European Union.

---

[16] https://www.w3.org/WoT/IG/.

References

1. Zanella, A., Bui, N., Castellani, A., Vangelista, L., Zorzi, M.: Internet of things for smart cities. IEEE Internet Things J. **1**(1), 22–32 (2014)
2. Huebscher, M.C., McCann, J.A.: A survey of autonomic computing degrees, models, and applications. ACM Comput. Surv. **40**, 1–28 (2008)
3. Kephart, J., Chess, D.: The vision of autonomic computing. Computer **36**, 41–50 (2003)
4. Wu, Q., Ding, G., Xu, Y., Feng, S., Du, Z., Wang, J., Long, K.: Cognitive internet of things: a new paradigm beyond connection. IEEE Internet Things J. **1**, 129–143 (2014)
5. Christophe, B., Boussard, M., Lu, M., Pastor, A., Toubiana, V.: The web of things vision: things as a service and interaction patterns. Bell Labs Tech. J. **16**, 55–61 (2011)
6. Al-Fuqaha, A., Khreishah, A., Guizani, M., Rayes, A., Mohammadi, M.: Toward better horizontal integration among IoT services. IEEE Commun. Mag. **53**(9), 72–79 (2015)
7. Alaya, M.B., Medjiah, S., Monteil, T., Drira, K.: Toward semantic interoperability in oneM2M architecture. IEEE Commun. Mag. **53**, 35–41 (2015)
8. Poslad, S., Middleton, S.E., Chaves, F., Tao, R., Necmioglu, O., Bugel, U.: A semantic IoT early warning system for natural environment crisis management. In: IEEE Transactions on Emerging Topics in Computing, vol. 3, jun 2015
9. Henson, C., Sheth, A., Thirunarayan, K.: Semantic perception: Converting sensory observations to abstractions. In: IEEE Internet Computing, vol. 6, no. 2 (2012)
10. Alaya, M.B., Banouar, Y., Monteil, T., Chassot, C., Drira, K.: OM2M: extensible ETSI-compliant M2M service platform with self-configuration capability. Procedia Comput. Sci. **32**, 1079–1086 (2014)
11. Corcho, O., García-Castro, R.: Five challenges for the semantic sensor web. Semant. Web **1**(1), 121–125 (2010)

A Framework to Support Interoperability in IoT and Facilitate the Development and Deployment of Highly Distributed Cloud Applications

Nikos Koutsouris[✉], Apostolos Voulkidis, and Kostas Tsagkaris

WINGS ICT Solutions, 336 Syggrou Avenue, 17673 Athens, Greece
{nkouts,avoulkidis,ktsagk}@wings-ict-solutions.eu

Abstract. The constantly increased variety of available hardware and software solutions for the IoT sector is facilitating the development of novel applications, but at the same time the lack of standardized or widely accepted means of interaction, deployment and configuration is seriously hindering the IoT's potential. The ARCADIA framework is an application development paradigm that enables the cooperation between software components designed and implemented independently and using various technologies and platforms, so that they can form sophisticated, distributed, cloud applications.

Keywords: Highly distributed applications · Microservice · Cloud · Unikernel · Virtualization · DevOps · Reconfiguration · SDN · Annotations

1 Introduction

The emerging era of cloud applications has already started and the concepts of IoT are ready to be introduced in the modern everyday life through the deployment of a large scope of novel applications, ranging from wearables, personal health and home automation, to smart city solutions, public safety and transportation. During the last years there is a proliferation of available hardware and software solutions related to IoT, which on one hand is definitely positive, but on the other hand, it has increased complexity in the IoT ecosystem, due to the low level of standardization and the lack of widely accepted means of interaction. This is something justifiable and actually expected, since manufacturers, as well as application providers, need to diversify, innovate and minimize time-to-market while developing their products. As for the caused heterogeneity, it can be compensated and hidden if a framework encompassing intelligent functions is used, like the one presented in the following.

The ARCADIA framework, which is developed in the ARCADIA project [1] and is funded by the H2020 EU programme, is a novel application development paradigm that enables the management of applications' configuration in a smart and dynamic way, allowing the combination of software components designed and implemented independently and using various technologies and platforms. The proposed framework addresses the challenge of interoperability by introducing the Smart Controller,

© ICST Institute for Computer Sciences, Social Informatics and Telecommunications Engineering 2017
N. Mitton et al. (Eds.): InterIoT 2016/SaSeIot 2016, LNICST 190, pp. 41–48, 2017.
DOI: 10.1007/978-3-319-52727-7_6

which incorporates several functionalities that can ensure the trustworthy interworking of components, based on an extensible context model that describes requirements and available options.

More information on the role and the modules of the Smart Controller is provided in Sect. 2.2. Beforehand, Sects. 1.1 and 1.2 highlight in brief the main concepts and technologies behind ARCADIA, while Sect. 2.1 introduces the basic parts of the ARCADIA ecosystem. Section 3 provides details on the steps required to develop a component, generate an application by chaining various components and then configure and deploy the application on the available infrastructure. Finally there are some conclusions on how the work should evolve in the mid and the long term. It has to be noted that this paper presents the current work in progress in the context of the ARCADIA project and all the described concepts will be elaborated and validated in a set of selected use cases before the first official release of the ARCADIA framework.

1.1   Virtualization and Cloudification

Virtualization refers to the act of creating a virtual (rather than actual) version of something, including, but not limited to, virtual computer hardware platforms, storage devices, and computer network resources [2]. It enables the optimized utilization of resources, as more applications and services can be packed onto the infrastructure. On the other hand, cloud computing offers through a broad network access, a pool of resources that can be assigned dynamically and on demand, while their usage can be monitored, controlled and optimized. To fully exploit the merits deriving from a virtualized cloud environment, it is required to go further than just porting applications and services from running on bare metal to running on Virtual Machines (VMs). Technologies such as containers and unikernels allow better resource and service management by further exploiting the concept of autonomous applications and micro-services. Unikernels are highly optimised, specialised machine images constructed by only using the minimum required set of operating system libraries to run an application. Their small footprint is an important feature for a cloud application as it reduces the cost of the deployment by using only minimal resources and increases the security of the application by shrinking the attack surface. Moreover, the lack of unnecessary operating system libraries allow unikernels to boot extremely fast making them ideal for mission critical or highly available applications.

One of the most difficult and expensive tasks on legacy, monolithic applications is scaling. Using design paradigms for cloud applications such as micro-service architecture, applications can be scaled up or down in a matter of seconds without extreme differences in cost. Modular applications consisting of several stateless micro-services are perfect for scaling operations and cost-effective deployment due to their autonomous nature. By separating data and functionality developers or service providers can easily scale out just a part of their application by deploying more instances of said micro services. In addition, stateless micro-services are more agile and fault tolerant which is vital requirement for highly distributed cloud applications.

Related work is carried out in the INPUT project [3] which aims at designing a novel infrastructure and paradigm to support Future Internet personal cloud services in a more scalable and sustainable way. The INPUT technologies intend to enable next-generation cloud applications to go beyond classical service models, and even to replace physical Smart Devices, usually placed in users' homes (e.g., set-top-boxes, etc.) or deployed around for monitoring purposes (e.g., sensors), with their virtual images, providing them to users "as a Service."

1.2 Management and Orchestration

In the era of cloud applications and micro-services, the ability to deliver complex and agile applications is getting harder and harder. Such applications should be Reconfigurable-by-Design, infrastructure independent and at the same time, resilient to failures and easily scalable. To overcome these difficulties, management tools are trying to simplify the deployment and scaling process by automating different aspects of the work-flow. Service modeling tools, like Juju [4], enable developers and IT professionals to automate mundane tasks and reduce workloads, by undertaking a big part of the deployment process on a private or public cloud. Developers can use such tools to create the blueprint of their application called "service graph", where they can define how micro-services are interacting with each other and have a general view of application data-flow. Moreover, DevOps environments are getting more and more difficult to manage due to the multiple Infrastructure as a Service (IaaS) providers.

Deploying a complex, service-based application on top of different infrastructures involves more complicated tasks, like network management, that require more sophisticated tools and frameworks. Apart from service modeling issues, different IaaS providers mean different network requirements and configurations as well as different policies. New development paradigms are trying to tackle such issues by leveraging the power of software defined networks and virtualized network functions. Application orchestration and network orchestration is an important requirement for cloud management tools and frameworks.

A related open-source system for automating deployment, scaling, and management of containerized applications is Kubernetes [5]. It groups containers that make up an application into logical units for easy management and discovery. It also supports self-healing of containers, service discovery and load balancing, horizontal scalability, batch execution and automated rollouts and rollbacks of application configurations. Finally, it is able to orchestrate storage and allow the seamless mounting of local storage, a public cloud provider or a network storage system.

2 The ARCADIA Platform

The ARCADIA framework [6] is a novel reconfigurable-by-design Highly Distributed Applications (HDA) development paradigm. It takes care of multi-infrastructure deployment, high availability requirements and automatic real-time reconfiguration of applications. To solve such issues, ARCADIA applications are based on a micro-service model and are governed by a sophisticated policy manager. In other words, each ARCADIA application consists of several autonomous components, which can communicate with each other based on a service graph and policy rules defined by the developers. Each component can be stored in a public or private registry on the ARCADIA platform and it can be re-used on other applications. To create an ARCADIA component, developers can transform their legacy applications by either using specific JAVA annotations if applications are java-based, or by wrapping them using java interfaces.

JAVA annotations are used to provide meta-data to a java application, without affecting the execution of the application itself, although they can be used for that as well. They are pre-defined words preceded by the "@" symbol and they can be written in many different parts of the code depending on their configuration, for example whether they annotate methods, classes, fields, etc. Annotations are used during three stages of the application life-cycle determined by their defined retention policy; before compilation, during build time or on runtime. Most of the natively supported annotations are discarded during compilation stage; however, ARCADIA annotations are configured to stay past that stage and during runtime. Using the Reflection API, provided by JAVA, the ARCADIA Smart Controller can read those annotations and give instructions to the application.

The ARCADIA Smart Controller consists of several modules such as the unikernel generator, the deployment manager and the policy manager. The Smart Controller is the heart of the framework and its responsibilities include, among others, network management, policy enforcement and annotation processing.

2.1   Architecture of the ARCADIA Ecosystem

As depicted in Fig. 1, the ARCADIA Smart Controller and the repository of the ARCADIA components form a platform that is managing the configuration, deployment, monitoring and potential reconfiguration of applications according to policies set by developers, application providers or IaaS providers. Developers create and push their components to the ARCADIA registry, where they can publish them with public or private access, according to the ARCADIA context model [7]. They can use all publicly available components to create a service graph for the application through an innovative web-based user interface. The deployment module creates the underlying Software Defined Network on top of different IaaS providers according to the policies and the requirements of the components that comprise the application.

2.2   The Role of the Smart Controller

The Smart Controller (SC) is the most sophisticated module of the framework. It contains several sub-modules that are important for many aspects of the applications life-cycle from the development to monitoring and reconfiguration. Starting from the development, SC is responsible for interpretation of annotation usage in a component, finding and deploying the required dependencies of a component and finally generating the unikernel which is the purposed-build virtual machine image for cloud deployment. Smart Controller is infrastructure agnostic and can deploy applications on different

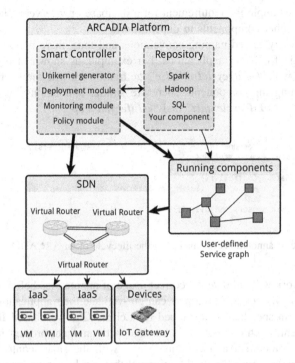

Fig. 1. Graphical representation of the ARCADIA ecosystem, illustrating also the main modules of the Smart Controller

infrastructure providers according to the policies defined by the developers. Moreover, by monitoring the components, Smart Controller is responsible for scaling and reconfiguring the application with complex optimization algorithms.

3   The ARCADIA Development Paradigm

ARCADIA framework doesn't force developers to re-write their existing applications from scratch, since by using specific JAVA annotations they can quickly convert a stand-alone application to an ARCADIA-compatible component.

3.1   Creating an ARCADIA Component

In order to have a valid ARCADIA component, a minimum of four JAVA annotations have to be used in the application; "*@ArcadiaComponent*" that declares the name and the version of the component and three more that define the life-cycle management methods to be called by the Smart Controller; however, developers can use as many annotations as their application requires in order to offer metrics or configuration parameters. Moreover, developers can use annotations that define dependencies of the component, for example the requirement for a database or vice versa the definition of an interface for other components to depend on it.

There aren't any forced naming conventions and thus, there is no need for heavy code refactoring of existing applications. For example, as shown in Fig. 2, by annotating a method with "*@LifecycleInitialize*" the framework will know which method to call before starting the component. There are similar annotations for start and stop functions namely "*@LifecycleStart*" and "*@LifecycleStop*".

```
@ArcadiaComponent(componentname="myIoTController", componentversion="1.0.0")
public class GatewayController{
    // … Private/public fields
    public GatewayController() {/*...*/}
    /** Initialize sensor attributes, establish sensor-gateway connections, etc */
    @LifecycleInitialize
    public void sensorsInitialization(){ /*...*/}
}
```

Fig. 2. Use of annotations for managing the lifecycle of an ARCADIA component

The framework will validate the correct usage of annotations before generating the final component. Moreover, developers can pre-validate their application by using the ARCADIA plugin specifically developed for Eclipse Che web based IDE [8] during their development. Each component is bundled with an agent process responsible for controlling the component and communicating with the smart controller. The final component is either a purposed-build unikernel that can be run under a hypervisor on any cloud infrastructure or a simple application that can be run on bare-metal machines like a raspberry Pi, ideal for IoT usage. Currently, ARCADIA supports virtual machines and unikernels but it can be easily extended to support bare-metal deployments. For the scope of this project, devices must be powerful enough to host a Java Virtual Machine (JVM).

3.2   Generating an Application Service Graph

One of the main issues with IoT applications is the huge variety of hardware and software vendors, and more specifically the consumption of the different data types each of them produces. With the ARCADIA framework, a component running on an IoT gateway can consume data from different sensors, and then offer them as metrics to the ARCADIA platform or provide an interface for other components to access them, by using simple annotations.

Developers can then use these datasets in any way their application requires, for example store them in a database or create a pipeline for Big Data analysis. In addition, various public components will be available through the ARCADIA registry and can be easily added to the service graph of the application. Moreover, an advanced policy editor is part of the framework where developers can configure different aspects of their application and let the Smart Controller handle the requirements, like high-availability of a component.

3.3   Configuration and Deployment Process

Configuring how individual components will communicate and interact with each other is a challenging task, considering the different architectures of infrastructure providers. To solve such issues, ARCADIA creates a virtual, infrastructure independent network on top of Open Overlay Router and offers a juju-like, service graph manager. Through this manager, developers can visualize or reconfigure the service graph of their application, add or remove components with a simple "drag and drop" and create a workflow for their application. Moreover, they can create complex graphs required by many applications like Big Data clusters, and pass data through virtual functions. The Smart Controller is responsible for deploying each component, and its dependencies, according to the policies defined by either the developer or the infrastructure provider and report any possible graph error, like graph loops.

4   Conclusions

Internet of Things applications can take advantage of the different features of the ARCADIA framework. For example, by using policies, metrics and re-configuration parameters, developers can control IoT devices like actuators or motors through the gateway component. Moreover, the exploitation of the annotations for discovering in the ARCADIA repository components that are necessary for implementing an application, multiplies the available options for developers; the necessary adaptations for ensuring interoperability are responsibility of the Smart Controller, which will set the optimal configuration through the ARCADIA agent of the object under control.

Till the end of the project, quantitative information on the network overhead and on aspects related to networking, like the bandwidth or latency requirements, will be published.

Moreover, in the remaining duration of the project, the developed functionalities of the Smart Controller will be tested and evaluated. In addition they will be enriched with knowledge building capabilities so as to further improve their performance. The Policy Management and Service Chaining parts will also be finalized and a fully functional release is planned to be made available for download by the end of 2017.

Acknowledgment. The work described in this paper is being performed within the ARCADIA project and has received funding from the European Community's Horizon 2020 Programme under grant agreement no. 645372.

References

1. The ARCADIA Horizon 2020 Project. http://arcadia-framework.eu/
2. Wikipedia. http://en.wikipedia.org/wiki/Virtualization
3. The INPUT Horizon 2020 Project. http://www.input-project.eu/
4. Juju Orchestrator by Canonical Ltd. https://jujucharms.com/about
5. Kubernetes system. http://kubernetes.io/

6. ARCADIA Horizon 2020 Project, deliverable D2.3 – Description of the ARCADIA Framework. http://www.arcadia-framework.eu/documentation/deliverables/
7. ARCADIA Horizon 2020 Project, deliverable D2.2 – Definition of the ARCADIA Context Model. http://www.arcadia-framework.eu/documentation/deliverables/
8. Eclipse Che Next-Generation IDE. http://www.eclipse.org/che/

F-Interop – Online Platform of Interoperability and Performance Tests for the Internet of Things

Sébastien Ziegler[1(✉)], Serge Fdida[2], Cesar Viho[3],
and Thomas Watteyne[3]

[1] Mandat International, Geneva, Switzerland
sziegler@mandint.org
[2] University Pierre and Marie Currie, Paris, France
serge.fdida@lip6.fr
[3] Inria, Paris, France
Cesar.Viho@irisa.fr, thomas.watteyne@inria.fr

Abstract. This article presents an initial set of results from the F-Interop European research project researching online platform for interoperability and performance tests for the Internet of Things. It presents some of the challenges faced by the IoT and online testing, and how F-Interop is addressing them, in order to provide an extensive experimental platform for online tests. It gives an overview of its overall architecture.

Keywords: Internet of Things · Tests · Testbed as a service · Interoperability · Conformance · Performance · Scalability · Privacy

1 Introduction and Project Presentation

The Internet of Things (IoT) is recognized as being the next technological revolution impacting all application domains. It will be massive and pervasive, with 50 to 100 Billion smart things and objects connected by 2020. Its role will be transversal and will impact diverse application domains, including: smart cities, agriculture, industries, eHealth, etc.

Since 1995, the interoperability is recognized by the International Telecommunication Union (ITU) as being the main obstacle to IoT development and adoption by the market. The success of this new technological revolution will hence be closely related to its capacity to overcome its current fragmentation. It will require supporting adequate standardization and interoperability.

F-Interop (www.f-interop.eu) [1] is a European research project addressing this challenge, by researching and developing an online platform of interoperability and performance testing tools for the IoT.

2 Problematic

In order to be widely adopted, new technologies, products and solutions go through several steps:

© ICST Institute for Computer Sciences, Social Informatics and Telecommunications Engineering 2017
N. Mitton et al. (Eds.): InterIoT 2016/SaSeIot 2016, LNICST 190, pp. 49–55, 2017.
DOI: 10.1007/978-3-319-52727-7_7

- Standardization: stakeholders discuss and align their views to converge towards common standards and specifications.
- Conformance & Interoperability: stakeholders test and validate that their implementation is conform to the standard.
- Optimization: in terms of Quality of Service, scalability, energy consumption, etc.
- Market Launch: the solution is ready for roll-out into the market.

Each phase traditionally requires extensive testing, where different vendors meet face-to-face to test interoperability by going through an exhaustive list of "interoperability tests". The consequence is that:

- The current process is extremely labor-intensive, as engineers travel across the globe often only to find out what they need to make a minor fix;
- The cost associated with engineering time and travel expenses is often too high for SMEs;
- Time-to-market is unnecessarily stretched, giving vendors who want to adopt emerging standards a disadvantage compared to vendors who come to market with entirely proprietary solutions.

F-Interop is leveraging on the European FIRE research infrastructure to develop online and remote interoperability and performance test tools supporting emerging technologies from research to standardization and to market launch. The outcome will be a set of tools enabling:

- Standardization communities to save time and resources, to be more inclusive with partners who cannot afford travelling, and to accelerate standardization processes;
- SMEs and companies to develop standards-based interoperable products with a time-to-market cut by 6–12 months, and significantly lowered engineering/financial overhead.

3   Technical Approach and Outcomes

The goal of F-Interop is extending FIRE+ with online interoperability and performance test tools supporting emerging IoT-related technologies from research to standardization and to market launch for the benefit of researchers, product development by SME, and standardization processes. Specifically, F-Interop will combine three complementary approaches:

Online Testing Tools. First and foremost, F-Interop is researching and developing online testing tools for the IoT, enabling to test interoperability, conformance, scalability, Quality of Service (QoS), the Quality of Experience (QoE), and energy efficiency of IoT devices and services.

Testbeds federations with a shared "Testbed as a Service". F-Interop brings together 3 testbed federations and facilities, encompassing over 32 testbeds and over 4'7000 IoT nodes, with:

- Fed4FIRE, which federates 24 FIRE+ testbeds, bringing together cloud, IoT, wireless, wireless mobile, LTE, cognitive radio, 5G, openflow, SDN, NFV and network emulation technologies.
- OneLab, which federates testbeds for the future Internet, including IoT, cognitive radio, wireless and overlay network technologies
- IoT Lab, which federates IoT and crowdsourcing/crowd-sensing testbeds, including smart campus, smart building and smart office testbeds.

In order to support this integration, F-Interop is extending the testbeds federation architecture model with a new layer enabling shared services among several testbed federations. This approach enables to interface "Testbed as a Service" (TBaaS) with existing federations through a clearly specified API, enabling remote access and interaction with various experimental platforms.

Support and to IoT Standardization and Industry. F-Interop works in close collaboration with several standardization bodies, and is directly contributing to three IoT standardization processes: oneM2M, 6TiSCH (IETF) and the Web of Things (W3C). It will also explore the possibility to support and enable new online certification and labelling mechanisms such as the IPv6 Ready logo. More generally, F-Interop intends to enable an easier participation of researchers and industry in standardization processes. It will also run an open call for SMEs and developers, inviting them to use and enrich the platform with additional modules and extensions.

Flexible Testing Schemes. F-Interop is researching and exploring various testing schemes and configurations, by interconnecting devices under tests with the server testing tools, resources provided by the F-Interop connected federations of testbeds, and resources provided by other users, as illustrated in Fig. 1, where the salmon hexagon represents a device under test.

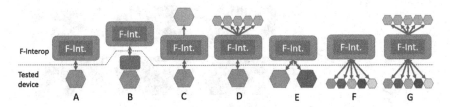

Fig. 1. Multiple testing schemes

4   Initial Architecture and Approach

The initial architecture has been designed by leveraging on the experience acquired by the three federations of testbeds participating in the project. It provides an additional layer of Testbed as a Service, on top of the three federations. But rather than a super federation, F-Interop should be considered as an autonomous testbed as a service with specific testing tools exploiting resources from the federated testbeds. Indeed, F-Interop is interested only in using relevant and targeted IoT resources (Fig. 2).

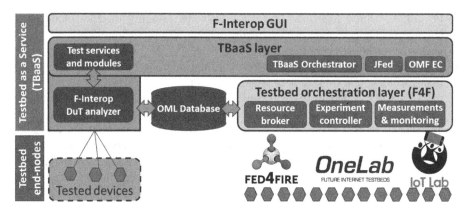

Fig. 2. Initial architectural view.

F-Interop-Platform distinguishes two main types of participants: F-Interop-Contributor and F-Interop-User. An F-Interop-Contributor (FI-Contributor) is any entity that provides testing tools into the F-Interop-Platform as well as testbeds and devices that are added to extend the existing testbeds. An F-Interop-User (FI-User) is any person or entity that has an IoT device, system or application to be tested (called IUT, Implementation Under Test) and wants to use the F-Interop-Platform to test it (Fig. 3).

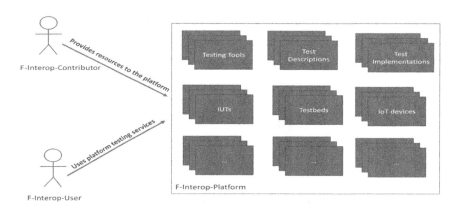

Fig. 3. F-Interop main components

We have considered the two types of testing tools that the F-Interop has to deal with: Online Interoperability testing and Online performance testing. We decided to select some of the targeted emerging IoT technologies that cover as many layers/aspects as possible of the IoT protocol stack. We decided to focus first on the two following protocols: 6TiSCH and CoAP. We have investigated the state of the art (existing methods and tools) for testing, and we have studied and compared existing IoT related testing solutions and tools.

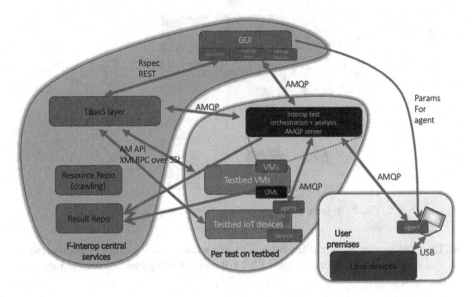

Fig. 4. F-Interop general architecture

Based on the test scenarios that have been developed and used during previous and recent interoperability face-to-face (F2F) interoperability testing events, we started studying what is needed for doing the same but in an online and remote manner. This work helped us in identifying key requirements and main components for online remote testing, as well as F-Interop-User and F-Interop-Contributor needs for running online remote testing. This work led to the definition of the first version of the overall architecture below (Fig. 4).

The following architecture has been defined more specifically for the case of remote online interoperability testing. It allows distinguishing the control plane in charge of managing the interactions between components and the data plane in charge of the test execution itself. Based on this architecture, a first proof of concept has been developed and authorizes CoAP online remote interoperability testing. The corresponding demo has been selected to be presented at the 25th Edition of the European Conference on Networks and Communications conference (EuCNC) in Athens, Greece, June 27-30, 2016. The proof of concept for 6TISCH and for oneM2M are under development (Fig. 5).

The remaining challenges to be addressed are synthesized as follow:

- To define a clear API enabling the interconnection of F-Interop as a service with the various testbed federations (or federated testbeds).
- To develop the targeted online testing tools: interoperability, conformance, and performance tests.
- To develop a generic and modular platform with an API enabling to extend the interoperability and conformance testing tools to new protocols and standards, including by voluntary third parties (FI-Contributors) or selected through the open call.

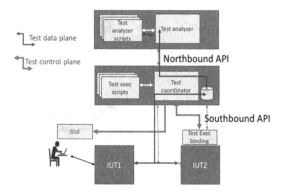

Fig. 5. F-Interop online interoperability testing architecture

- To develop a generic and modular platform with an API enabling various testing tool modules integration, including by voluntary third parties or selected through the open call.

5   Conclusions – Towards Online Interop and Performance Tests

In order to support the IoT research, development and industrial exploitation, F-Interop is developing a platform of online testing tools encompassing interoperability, compliance and performance tests. It is progressing towards a new model of interop test, enabling a larger participation with remote ad distributed tests.

The F-Interop platform is still in its development phase. However, it already announces an open call with funding to develop new partnerships with third parties research projects interested to develop complementary testing tools, address additional standards and/or organize F-Inerop based interop tests in standardization processes. More information is available on the project website at: www.f-interop.eu.

Acknowledgments. This article has been written in the context of the F-Interop European research project of the Horizon 2020 Framework Program supported by the European Commission. It is implemented by a consortium coordinated by UPMC and Mandat International. F-Interop project also capitalized on other projects results, including IoT Lab, Fed4FIRE, and OneLab.

References

1. IoT Lab is a European research project from the FP7 research programme. http://www.iotlab.eu
2. Open Systems Interconnection model developed by the International Standardization Orgaization: ISO/IEC 7498-1:1994. http://www.iso.org
3. University of Surrey. http://www.surrey.ac.uk

4. Mandat International. http://www.mandint.org
5. University of Geneva. http://www.unige.ch
6. CTI - Computer Technology Institute and Press "Diophantus". http://www.cti.gr
7. Smart Santanders. http://www.smartsantander.eu
8. Future Internet research in the ICT Programme. http://www.ict-fire.eu
9. Fed4FIRE is the main project aiming at federating European research testbeds. http://www.fed4fire.eu
10. OneLab. https://onelab.eu/
11. Postel, J.: Internet Protocol, RFC 791, Internet Engineering Task Force RFC 791, September 1981
12. Internet Protocol, Version 6 (IPv6), RFC 2460, IETF. https://www.ietf.org/rfc/rfc2460.txt
13. Ericson white paper 284 23-3149 Uen | February 2011, More than 50 billion connected devices. http://www.ericsson.com/res/docs/whitepapers/wp-50-billions.pdf
14. UDG is an IPv6-based multi-protocol control and monitoring system using IPv6 as a common identifier for devices using legacy protocols. It was developed by a Swiss research project and used by IoT6 for research purpose. More information on UDG ongoing developments. www.devicegateway.com
15. Available. http://www.turnitipv6.com
16. IoT6 European research project. http://www.iot6.eu
17. Ziegler, S., Crettaz, C., Ladid, L., Krco, S., Pokric, B., Skarmeta, A.F., Jara, A., Kastner, W., Jung, M.: IoT6 – moving to an IPv6-Based future IoT. In: Galis, A., Gavras, A. (eds.) FIA 2013. LNCS, vol. 7858, pp. 161–172. Springer, Heidelberg (2013). doi:10.1007/978-3-642-38082-2_14
18. Ziegler, S., Thomas, I.: IPv6 as a global addressing scheme and integrator for the Internet of Things and the Cloud
19. Ziegler, S., Palattella, M.R., Ladid, L., Krco, S., Skarmeta, A.: Scalable integration framework for heterogeneous smart objects, applications and services. In: Internet of Things – From Research and Innovation to Market Deployment. River Publishers Series in Communication (2014)
20. Ziegler, S., Hazan, M., Xiaohong, H., Ladid, L.: IPv6-based test beds integration across Europe and China. In: Testbeds and Research Infrastructure: Development of Networks and Communities (2014)
21. UDG is maintained by the UDG Alliance managed by Device Gateway and has been used by several European research projects, including Hobnet, IoT6, EAR-IT and currently by IoT Lab. http://www.devicegateway.com
22. The application will be made available on the IoT Lab website. http://www.iotlab.eu
23. ITU Focus Group on Smart Sustainable Cities. http://www.itu.int/en/ITU-T/focusgroups/ssc/Pages/default.aspx
24. World Summit on the Information Society (2015). http://www.itu.int/net4/wsis/forum/2015/

Guard Time Optimisation for Energy Efficiency in IEEE 802.15.4-2015 TSCH Links

Georgios Z. Papadopoulos[2(✉)], Alexandros Mavromatis[1], Xenofon Fafoutis[1], Robert Piechocki[1], Theo Tryfonas[1], and George Oikonomou[1]

[1] Faculty of Engineering, University of Bristol, Bristol, UK
{a.mavromatis,xenofon.fafoutis,r.j.piechocki,theo.tryfonas,
g.oikonomou}@bristol.ac.uk
[2] IRISA, Télécom Bretagne, Institut Mines-Télécom, Paris, France
georgios.papadopoulos@telecom-bretagne.eu

Abstract. Time Slotted Channel Hopping (TSCH) is among the Medium Access Control (MAC) schemes defined in the IEEE 802.15.4-2015 standard. TSCH aims to guarantee high-level network reliability by keeping nodes time-synchronised. In order to ensure successful communication between a sender and a receiver, the latter starts listening shortly before the expected time of a MAC layer frame's arrival. The offset between the time a node starts listening and the estimated time of frame arrival is called guard time and it aims to reduce the probability of missed frames due to clock drift. In this paper, we investigate the impact of the guard time length on network performance. We identify that, when using the 6TiSCH minimal schedule, the most significant cause of energy consumption is idle listening during guard time. Therefore, we perform empirical optimisations on the guard time to maximise the energy-efficiency of a TSCH link. Our experiments, conducted using the Contiki OS, show that optimal guard time configuration can reduce energy consumption by up to 40%, without compromising network reliability.

Keywords: Internet of Things · IEEE 802.15.4-2015 · TSCH · Synchronisation · Guard time · Performance evaluation · Energy consumption

1 Introduction

In 2016 the IEEE 802.15.4-2015 standard [1] was published to offer a certain quality of service for deterministic industrial-type applications. Among the operating modes defined in this standard, Time-Slotted Channel Hopping (TSCH) is a Medium Access Control (MAC) protocol for low-power and reliable networking solutions in Low-Power Lossy Networks (LLNs). Although there is a vast literature of unstandardised MAC protocols that are optimised for different scenarios [2], the standardised TSCH offers interoperability between IoT devices. TSCH specifies a channel hopping scheme to avoid interference, and consequently to enable high reliability [3], while it employs time synchronisation to achieve

© ICST Institute for Computer Sciences, Social Informatics and Telecommunications Engineering 2017
N. Mitton et al. (Eds.): InterIoT 2016/SaSeIot 2016, LNICST 190, pp. 56–63, 2017.
DOI: 10.1007/978-3-319-52727-7_8

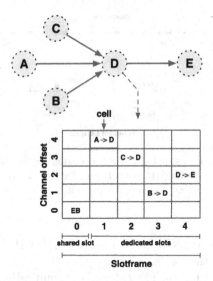

Fig. 1. An example TSCH schedule for node D. $A > D$ stands for "node A sends to node D", while EB cells are used for broadcast and advertisement frames.

low-power operation (Fig. 1). TSCH presents a deterministic scheduling app-roach where each cell consists of a pair of a timeslot and a channel offset for collision avoidance purposes. Each channel offset is translated into a frequency through a function that uses as input the ASN (Absolute Sequence Number) and the number of available frequencies (e.g., 16 when using IEEE 802.15.4-compliant radios at 2.4 GHz with all channels in use) [4].

To account for loss of synchronisation, a TSCH receiver maintains its radio on receiving mode for an extended period of time, named Guard Time. In [5], we highlighted the effect of guard time on network performance. We identified that, when employing the 6TiSCH minimal schedule, most of the energy consumed is wasted in idle listening, due to the guard time. In this paper, we further investigate the importance of guard time optimisation. To this aim, we study using both an analytical model and simulations the optimal guard time as a function of the clock drift. Our performance evaluation results using the Cooja simulator, demonstrate that fine-tuning the guard time, under realistic clock drift configurations (e.g., 20 ppm, 30 ppm), can significantly improve the energy efficiency of a TSCH link without compromising its reliability.

2   TSCH Overview

Under the TSCH scheme, nodes periodically exchange Enhanced Beacon (EB) packets to remain time-synchronised throughout the network's lifetime. Synchro-nisation does not need explicit EB exchange, data packets may also be utilised to compute clock drifts [6]. Typically, an EB contains time and channel frequency information, as well as information about the initial link and slotframe for new

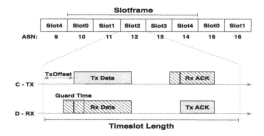

Fig. 2. A typical TSCH timeslot template for a transmitter (top) and receiver node (bottom): node C, transmits its data packet after `TxOffset`, while the receiver D, uses a `Guard Time` to avoid missing the incoming packet by turning its radio on slightly before the packet arrival.

nodes to join the network. New nodes may join a TSCH network by "hearing" an EB frame from another node.

Figure 2 illustrates a typical TSCH-based communication between two nodes. In TSCH networks, time is divided into timeslots of equal length, large enough to transmit a frame and to receive an acknowledgement, while a set of timeslots construct a slotframe. At each timeslot, a node may transmit or receive a frame, or it may turn its radio `off` for saving energy. Each timeslot can be either dedicated (contention-free) or shared (contention-based approach). Finally, each timeslot is labelled with `ASN`, a variable which counts the number of timeslots since the network was established, `ASN` is initialised to 0.

A node transmits a data packet at the beginning of each timeslot, exactly after the `TxOffset`. TSCH incorporates a `Guard Time` to account for loss of synchronisation. To account for both positive and negative clock drift, the receiver wakes up before the expected end of the `TxOffset` and keeps the radio on for τ seconds or until a frame preamble is received. The guard time τ is equally spaced around the end of the `TxOffset`. Thus, for a certain guard time, τ, the maximum synchronisation error, ϵ_τ, that can be tolerated is:

$$\epsilon_\tau = \frac{\tau}{2} - \tau_p, \tag{1}$$

where τ_p is the time required for the reception of the frame preamble. Let us consider the use of clocks with an error of $\pm e_f$. The synchronisation error accumulates over time. The worst case scenario for synchronisation is right before a synchronisation event (e.g., EB frame), when the error is:

$$\epsilon_T = T\left(\frac{1}{1 - e_f} - \frac{1}{1 + e_f}\right), \tag{2}$$

where T is the period of synchronisation events. By equating (1) and (2), we calculate a minimum guard time required to achieve zero packet loss due to loss of synchronisation (τ_m):

$$\tau_m = 2T\left(\frac{1}{1 - e_f} - \frac{1}{1 + e_f}\right) + 2\tau_p. \tag{3}$$

It can be observed that in the ideal case where the clock error is $e_f = 0$ ppm, the minimum acceptable guard time is $\tau_m = 2\tau_p$.

3 Performance Evaluation

In order to assess the impact of guard time in the performance of TSCH, we performed a set of experiments using Cooja, the network simulator distributed as part of the Contiki open-source operating system for the Internet of Things[1]. In our experiments we emulated Z1 motes. We conducted a large number of simulations under various realistic clock drifts (e.g., ±10, ±20 ppm). To account for the worst case scenario, we configured the transmitter node to the maximum positive clock drift and the receiver at the maximum negative drift. For instance, in the case of the ±20 ppm configuration, we set the transmitter node at +20 ppm and the receiver at −20 ppm, resulting to a relative drift of 40 ppm. The clock drifts are constant throughout each simulation. Furthermore, we performed simulations under different guard time (e.g., 400, 600 µs) configurations, while keeping the default values for the remaining parameters, such as EB or data packet transmission frequency.

3.1 Setup

For our evaluation we use a scenario with two nodes, one leaf transmitter and one sink receiver, positioned at a distance of 20 m. We choose the data packet size to be equal to 102 bytes that corresponds to all necessary information for MAC, routing and application operations. Furthermore, we use Cooja's Unit Disk Graph Medium (UDGM) radio model, with each node transmitting frames at 0 dBm. Lastly, each simulation lasted 60 min. Full details of the simulation setup are presented in Table 1.

3.2 Simulation Results

In [5], we studied the impact of idle listening during guard time on energy consumption. Hereinafter we discuss our proposed guard time optimisation and the gains that it can offer in terms of reliability, goodput and energy consumption.

Guard Time: We first investigate the minimum guard time, while guaranteeing 100% Packet Delivery Ratio (PDR), under different clock drift values (i.e., 0, ±10, ±20, ±30 *and* ±40 ppm) using both the analytical model and a set of simulations. Note that packet loss is calculated as $1 - PDR$, and thus, packet loss 0% is the equivalent of 100% PDR. As can be observed from Fig. 3a, Eq. (3) approximates a linear behaviour ($\tau_p = 129$ µs, $T = 1.71$ s), which is validated by the simulations. For instance, in case of a ±20 ppm drift, a typical worst-case clock drift in IoT-devices [8], 390 µs is the minimum guard time length

---

[1] Contiki OS - www.contiki-os.org.

Table 1. Simulation setup.

Topology parameters	Value
Number of nodes	2 (a transmitter and receiver)
Node spacing	20 m in a line topology
Simulation parameters	Value
Duration	60 min
Traffic pattern	1 frame/60 s
Data packet size	102 bytes (77 *bytes payload*)
Routing model	RPL [7]
MAC model	TSCH (6TiSCH minimal schedule)
TSCH parameters	Value
EB period	3.42 s
Slotframe length	7
Timeslot length	15 ms
Guard Time	$(0 - 2200)\,\mu s$
Clock Drift	$(0, \pm 10, \pm 20, \pm 30 \ and \ \pm 40)\,ppm$
Hardware parameters	Value
Antenna model	CC2420
Radio propagation	2.4 GHz
Transmission power	0 dBm

for operation without compromising network reliability due to loss of synchronisation or goodput (Fig. 3b). Note that both nodes operate as EB transmitters and receivers; thus, the link is synchronised at half the EB period on average, $T = 3.42/2 = 1.71$ s.

Energy Efficiency: To evaluate the energy consumption of each network node, we employed Contiki's `Powertrace` and `Energest` modules. These modules monitor and log the radio and Micro-Controller Unit (MCU) usage in real-time by tracking the time spent in various states (i.e., Radio transmitting or receiving, or sleeping). Table 2 provides typical current consumption levels at each of these states for the Z1 mote[2], under a 3 V operating voltage. Note that in this evaluation we focus on the energy consumption performance related with the radio communication only.

We here investigate the impact of guard time duration on energy consumption (± 20 ppm). To this aim, we first present energy consumption performance under various guard time configurations. Our results demonstrate that by reducing guard time (i.e., from 2200 μs, the default configuration of Contiki's TSCH implementation, to 400 μs), we can decrease the average power consumption per

---

[2] http://zolertia.sourceforge.net/wiki/images/e/e8/Z1_RevC_Datasheet.pdf.

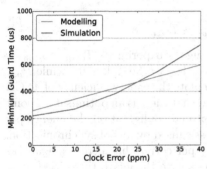 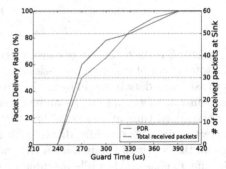

(a) Minimum guard time for operation (b) PDR & goodput performance under a
without packet loss.   ± 20 *ppm* clock drift.

Fig. 3. Minimum required guard time for various clock drifts (left) and the network
performance under ±20 ppm clock drift (right), values are in average.

Table 2. Approximate energy consumption of the Z1 mote.

IC	Notes	Current consumption
CC2420	TX mode @ 0 dBm	17.4 mA
	RX mode	18.8 mA
	Radio off mode	0.5 μA

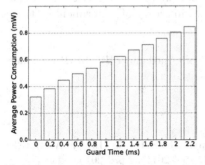 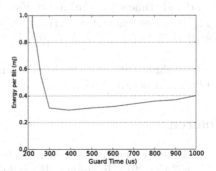

(a) Average power consumption, under dif- (b) Energy consumption per successful re-
ferent guard time durations.   ceived bit.

Fig. 4. A thorough power consumption performance of the TSCH scheme, under a
±20 ppm clock drift [8].

node (i.e., receiver node in our scenario) by more than 40%, (Fig. 4a). Energy
consumption is reduced further at guard times lower than 390 μs, yet at the
cost of compromising reliability. To better visualise this trade-off, we define the
energy-efficiency of TSCH as the average energy consumed for the successful
reception of a single bit, and it is calculated as follows:

$$\eta = \frac{E}{PDR * T_{transmissions} * P_{size} * 8} ,\tag{4}$$

where E is the total energy consumed during the experiment, $T_{transmissions}$ is the total count of frame transmissions from the leaf to the sink node, while P_{size} is the size of a data frame in bytes. Figure 4b plots the energy efficiency of TSCH as a function of guard time. It can be observed that there is an optimisation point for the guard time at $390\,\mu s$. Below that optimal configuration the energy per correct bit increases rapidly, due to packet loss caused by loss of synchronisation. Above that optimal configuration the energy per correct bit increases again, as the energy consumed in idle listening increases with the guard time.

4   Conclusion

In this work, we first investigated the impact of guard time on TSCH performance in terms of network reliability, goodput and energy consumption. We then performed empirical optimisations on the guard time to maximise the energy-efficiency of a TSCH link. Our performance evaluation results, using the Cooja simulator, demonstrate that the guard time has a straightforward impact on energy consumption. In particular, we have shown that fine-tuning the guard time can result into significant savings in energy consumption without compromising network reliability. Our ongoing work consists of further investigating this lead in multi-hop networks, where the clock drift may have a heavy impact on networkwide time synchronisation. Furthermore, we plan to study the behaviour of TSCH under realistic conditions by performing a set of experimental studies over the FIT IoT-LAB testbed [9].

Acknowledgements. This work was partially performed under IRC-SPHERE funded by EPSRC, Grant EP/K031910/1.

References

1. IEEE Standard for Low-Rate Wireless Personal Area Networks (LR-WPANs), IEEE Std 802.15.4-2015 (Revision of IEEE Std 802.15.4-2011), April 2016
2. Bachir, A., Dohler, M., Watteyne, T., Leung, K.: MAC essentials for wireless sensor networks. Commun. Surv. Tutorials **12**(2), 222–248 (2010)
3. Watteyne, T., Mehta, A., Pister, K.: Reliability through frequency diversity: why channel hopping makes sense. In: Proceedings of the 6th ACM Symposium on Performance Evaluation of Wireless Ad Hoc, Sensor, and Ubiquitous Networks, pp. 116–123 (2009)
4. Watteyne, T., Palattella, M., Grieco, L.: Using IEEE 802.15.4e Time-Slotted Channel Hopping (TSCH) in the Internet of Things (IoT): Problem Statement. RFC 7554 (2015)
5. Mavromatis, A., Papadopoulos, G.Z., Fafoutis, X., Elsts, A., Oikonomou, G., Tryfonas, T.: Impact of guard time length on IEEE 802.15.4e TSCH energy consumption. In: Proceedings of the IEEE International Conference on Sensing, Communication and Networking (SECON) (2016)

6. Chang, T., Watteyne, T., Pister, K., Wang, Q.: Adaptive synchronization in multi-hop TSCH networks. Comput. Netw. **76**, 165–176 (2015)
7. Winter, T., Thubert, P., Brandt, A., Hui, J., Kelsey, R., Levis, P., Pister, K., Struik, R., Vasseur, J., Alexander, R.: RPL: IPv6 routing protocol for low-power and lossy networks. RFC 6550 (2012)
8. Fafoutis, X., Janko, B., Mellios, E., Hilton, G., Sherratt, R.S., Piechocki, R., Craddock, I.: SPW-1: a low-maintenance wearable activity tracker for residential monitoring and healthcare applications. In: Proceedings of the EAI International Conference on Wearables in Healthcare (HealthWear) (2016)
9. Papadopoulos, G.Z., Beaudaux, J., Gallais, A., Noel, T., Schreiner, G.: Adding value to WSN simulation using the IoT-LAB experimental platform. In: Proceedings of the 9th IEEE International Conference on Wireless and Mobile Computing, Networking and Communications (WiMob), pp. 485–490 (2013)

SaSeIoT

On the Performance of Key Pre-distribution
for RPL-Based IoT Networks

Ayman El Hajjar[1]([⊠]), George Roussos[1], and Maura Paterson[2]

[1] Department of Computer Science and Information Systems,
Birkbeck, University of London, London, England
{a.elhajjar,g.roussos}@bbk.ac.uk
[2] Department of Economics, Mathematics and Statistics,
Birkbeck, University of London, London, England
m.paterson@bbk.ac.uk

Abstract. A core ingredient of the *Internet of Things (IoT)* is the use of deeply embedded resource constrained devices, often connected to the Internet over Low Power and Lossy Networks. These constraints compounded by the need for unsupervised operation within an untrusted environment create considerable challenges for the secure operation of these systems. In this paper, we propose a novel method to secure an edge IoT network using the concept of key pre-distribution proposed by Eschenauer and Gligor in the context of distributed sensor networks. First, we investigate the performance of the unmodified algorithm in the Internet of Things setting and then analyse the results with a view to determine its performance and thus its suitability in this context. Specifically, we investigate how ring size influences performance in order to determine the required ring size that guarantees full connectivity of the network. We then proceed to propose a novel *RPL objective function* and associated metrics that ensure that any node that joins the network can establish secure communication with Internet destinations.

1 Introduction

In recent years, with the development of wireless sensor networks, the Internet of Things (IoT) became a reality. This presents many challenges that also did not exist before because of the nature of the IoT. Since the IoT is a collection of heterogeneous networks, it involves not only the same security problems with sensor network, but also more particular ones, such as privacy protection problem, heterogeneous network authentication and access control problems, information storage and management [1].

The research into the IoT security is far more complicated then that of the Internet security in general. Conventional security protocols for the Internet as we know are not suitable for the Internet of Things. Devices in the IoT are different in terms of computation capabilities, memory limitation, processing power and physical limitation (i.e., installed in rural area and unattended). Thus factors such as reliability, scalability, modularity, interoperability, interface and QoS can be hard to achieve [2].

© ICST Institute for Computer Sciences, Social Informatics and Telecommunications Engineering 2017
N. Mitton et al. (Eds.): InterIoT 2016/SaSeIot 2016, LNICST 190, pp. 67–78, 2017.
DOI: 10.1007/978-3-319-52727-7_9

Security of the Internet of Things is at the centre of research. The impact of security breaches on humans in an IoT device is much greater than in conventional networks. For example, a breach of a device monitoring the CO_2 level in a room can lead to physical harm to a human being if this device is compromised and is sending data that are not accurate. Thus authentication and authorization are key to ensuring that only authenticated devices (those that share a suitable key) can join the network. The main challenge, when it comes to authentication of various IoT devices, is the design of key storage and distribution mechanisms, because of the nature of the IoT devices and their network architecture [3].

Given the limitation that IoT devices (sensors and actuators) are constrained in term of computational power and storage memory, several of the conventional security methods are not suitable for use.

The purpose of this paper is to investigate the performance of Laurent Eschenauer and Virgil D. Gligor's Algorithm [4] for Distributed Sensor Networks (DSN) in the context of IPv6 Low Power and Lossy Networks (6LoW-PAN) Devices for the Internet of Things (IoT). We provide an analysis of the performance of the algorithm when applied in the DSN and IoT context. We also show the ring size needed to guarantee full network connectivity. We then propose a modification of the routing protocol for Low power and Lossy Networks (RPL) Objective function (OF) in order for the key pre-distribution algorithm to achieve a full network connectivity in the context of the IoT.

Section 2 provides an introduction to the Internet of Things, the 6LoWPAN network protocol, the IPv6 Routing Protocol for Low Power and Lossy Networks (RPL) and several solutions that attempts to secure the Internet of Things. Section 3 presents the key pre-distribution algorithm by Eschenauer and Gligor in [4]. In Sect. 4, we present the experiment methodology and design that we carried in order to first validate the results of [4] and second to determine whether those results are applicable in the context of the IoT. In Sect. 5 we provide an overview of the future work that will be carried on to enable key pre-distribution algorithm to become a suitable solution for the IoT. Finally, we present our main conclusions in Sect. 5.

2   Understanding the Problem: Literature Review

Distributed Sensor Networks (DSN) include a large array of sensor nodes that are usually battery powered, have limited computational capabilities and memory. Nodes in a DSN network, collect data and make it available for processing to application components of the network and control nodes. The scale of a DSN network is quite large (tens of thousands). The Internet of Things (IoT) network is a collection of sensor networks (Wireless and Distributed) that share the same characteristics as Distributed Sensor Networks.

2.1   Internet of Things and 6LoWPAN

Internet of Things is a simple low cost communication network that allows wireless connectivity in applications with limited power and relaxed throughput requirements [5]. 6LoWPAN concept originated from the idea that "the Internet Protocol could and should be applied even to the smallest devices" and that low-power devices with limited processing capabilities should be able to participate in the Internet of Things [6].

Internet protocols has always been considered too heavy for sensor networks and thus the 6LoWPAN protocol stacks were created. The need for an IP based sensor network made many researchers attempt to adapt existing Internet standards to the creation of interoperable protocols and the development of supporting mechanisms for composable services [7]. Not surprisingly, one of these challenges is security because of the distinct features of sensor networks such as the capabilities of the nodes. In Sect. 2.3, we will review the various attempts to create new security protocols for sensor networks and the IoT or to adapt existing protocols in the context of the IoT.

Given those limitations, another problem arises with IP for the 6LoWPAN network stacks that is relevant to this paper, the topology of the network. Various topologies should be supported by 6LoWPAN networks including mesh and star. Routing for Low Power and Lossy network (RPL) as described in [8], is a routing protocol for 6LoWPAN networks that can solve this problem.

2.2   Routing for Low Power and Lossy Networks RPL

The Routing Protocol for Low-Power and Lossy Networks (RPL) is a distance vector IPv6 routing protocol designed for LLN networks. RPL is designed for networks which comprise of thousands of nodes where the majority of the nodes have very constrained energy and/or channel capacity. To conserve precious resources, a routing protocol must generate control traffic sparingly. However, this is at odds with the need to quickly propagate any new routing information to resolve routing inconsistencies quickly.

RPL organises its topology in a Directed Acyclic Graph (DAG). An RPL DAG must have at least one RPL root and a Destination Oriented DAG (DODAG) is constructed for each root. The root acts as a sink for the topology by storing all routes to all nodes in the DODAG in the routing table. The root may also act as a border router for the DODAG to allow nodes that belong to different DODAGs to communicate [8].

RPL supports three security modes: unsecured, preinstalled and authenticated. Unsecured refers to the security mechanism that is provided in lower layers such as link layer security. Preinstalled and authenticated modes require the use of preinstalled shared keys on all nodes prior to deploying the nodes. Both modes provide security procedures and mechanisms at the conceptual level and are concerned with authentication, access control, data confidentiality, data integrity and non repudiation. This study focuses on the preinstalled mode as a method of securing message transmission between nodes in an RPL DAG instance.

Authentication in the preinstalled mode involves the mutual authentication of the routing peers prior to exchanging route information (i.e. peer authentication) as well as ensuring that the source of the route data is from the peer (i.e. data origin authentication) [9]. The limitation of the preinstalled mode in its common form, is that it is assumed that a node wishing to join a secured network is pre-configured with a shared key for all neighbours and the RPL root. This means that once this shared key is compromised, all network leaves in the RPL DODAG are compromised.

2.3 Security for the Internet of Things Proposed Solutions

Providing key management for confidentiality and group level authentication in a sensor network is difficult due to the ad hoc nature and limited resources of the distributed sensor network environment. The main challenge in public key algorithms when using in the context of Internet of Things, similarly to sensor networks, is the energy consumption of exchanging public key certificates [10].

Key management protocols can be divided into three categories. Arbitrated keying protocols, Self Enforcing protocols and Pre-Deployed Keying protocols.

Arbitrated keying protocols requires a trusted server such as the use of [11]. They are not suitable for use in the context of the IoT because of the limited energy, communication bandwidth and computational capacities of sensor nodes in an IoT network. The Otway-Rees protocol in [12] is applied in the context of the IoT for one-way authentication; symmetric cryptography with AES is used for encryption. The drawback in one way authentication is that it leaves the network vulnerable to man-in-the-middle attacks.

Self Enforcing protocols such as Pairwise Asymmetric Keying are based on the Diffie-Hellman key agreement protocol. A proposed solution to use a light-weight DTLS based keying mechanism to secure IoT was suggested in [13]. Although this solution proved to provide a lighter and robust security protocol using pairwise key establishment between nodes, the number of message transfers to establish the secure connection in [13] still introduced a large communication overhead. Pre-deployed keys into nodes prior to deployment in a network offers energy efficient solution to providing confidentiality and group level authentication keys [10].

In the next section we investigate the use of the key management scheme for Distributed Sensor Networks proposed by Eschenauer and Gligor in [4] in the context of the Internet of Things.

3   Key Pre Distribution as a Solution for Securing IoT

Offline key pre-distribution algorithm for DSN by Eschenauer and Gligor [4] describes the method by which keys are distributed to nodes in the network.

This key pre-distribution mechanism ensures that for each direct link between any two nodes in the network, the probability of those two sharing at least a key is 0.5. The authors of [4] concluded that the size of key rings and identifier rings $RING$ does not need to be large in order for a network to guarantee full connectivity and only 50% of those pair of nodes need to have a shared key.

At first, a large pool P of keys K and identifiers I is generated. Each key K in the pool is randomly represented by one of the identifiers I. A certain number of identifiers K and their respective keys K are picked from the pool P randomly and loaded into the memory of the node. This will form the key ring and the identifier ring. This step will be repeated for each node that wishes to join the network.

Now that each node in the network has an identifier ring and a key ring loaded into its memory, nodes can begin the phase of selecting a secure route to any other nodes. Each node broadcast its identifier ring to all neighbouring nodes (neighbouring nodes are the nodes that are within it is transmission range). Each neighbouring node compares the identifier ring it received with its own identifier ring. If the node find a shared identifier between the two identifier rings, it sends a message to the origin node with the shared identifier. Nodes that have a shared identifier can establish a secure direct link by using the key that corresponds to the shared identifier. Nodes that do not share an identifier with the origin node will attempt to create a link with it through other nodes (indirect links by hops).

An example in [4] showed that when a pool contained 100,000 keys, full network connectivity was achieved with only 75 keys in the rings. This is due to the fact that routing in Distributed Sensor Networks (DSN) allows multi hops and indirect hop communication between nodes, thus nodes that do no share an identifier can use another node that it shares an identifier with as an indirect link to reach it.

This paper is attempting to evaluate the performance of this algorithm in the context of the IoT environment when using RPL.

4   Experiment Design and Setup

The experiment was simulated on the Contiki Operating System [14] using Cooja nodes simulator [15]. A C program was coded to generate keys pool, IDs pool, Key rings, ID rings[1]. The simulation file was composed of N nodes and one border router[2]. A script was written in order for the simulation to stop running only when all possible routes were computed and no more routes exist. This was essential to ensure that the routing table we obtain at the end of each simulation is the optimum one for our setting. Finally, a Perl program was coded to analyse logs generated by individual nodes after simulation in order to determine if nodes were able to establish a secure link.

4.1   Experiment Parameters

The parameters selected for the simulation experiments aim to approximately match the characteristics of a recent innovative deployment of IoT technology at

---

[1] Keys & identifiers were generated randomly using Blum Blum Schub generator. Each node will then choose a set of Keys & identifiers for its key ring and identifier ring randomly using Knuth Shuffle algorithm.

[2] A border router is also the root of the RPL DODAG and it will store the routing table of the simulation (acting as a sink).

the campus of the University of Liverpool in the UK, where 650 students were able to employ a smartphone app to access discounts or coupons in stores or cafeterias, as well as for wayfinding and alerting. Specifically, the overall area of 250 × 250 meters which is a typical area size of a medium sized university campus. Number of users (Network size) is based on an average number of wifi usage at Birbkeck campus during a day which is 2394 users [17]. The main difference between out simulations and the use case we use for motivation is the wireless technology used which was Bluetooth Low Energy (BLE) while in the simulations we use Zigbee.

Parameters related to the environment (control parameters) of the simulation were defined in the experiment configuration. We assumed that the transmitting range for each node is 50 meters (this is the common transmitting range for 6LoWPAN low power devices). We also used the key length *klength* of 64 bits and the ID length *ilength* of 32 bits. Those two sizes were chosen as they are enough, given the number of nodes we simulated in the experiment. The number of bits in ID was chosen to be smaller because of memory constraints in the Internet of things devices. The other reason is that exchanging IDs is not revealing anything as there is no connection between keys and IDs is exchanged. Anyone trying to intercept the messages will not be able to make the connection between the identifier exchanged and the key it represents.

We carried out the experiment simulations with three different parameters (independent parameters) changing. The Pool size P of keys is the first parameter. Two pools are being generated in each simulation, one for keys, the other for IDs. Both have the same size. The pool size is an important factor that will have a huge impact on the probability of shared keys between motes. The pools size we run simulations for are: 100, 250, 500,750,1,000 and 2,500 motes. The second parameter is the network size N. The third parameter is the ring size RS It was computed using Stirling equation as per [4]. Those independent variables are shown below and in Table 1. For each pool size (P), keys and identifers are generated once for all networks size. To ensure the accuracy of experiment simulations, each simulation will run 5 times. The largest and smallest results were discarded and the average of the remaining three runs is used. The outputs of

Table 1. Independent variables

Pool size (P)	Ring size (RS)	Network size (N)					
100	8	100					
250	13	100	250				
500	18	100	250	500			
750	22	100	250	500	750		
1,000	25	100	250	500	750	1,000	
2,500	41	100	250	500	750	1,000	2,500

each of those experiments are the Number of DAGs $DAGs$ in the routing table and the Number of Shared Keys NSK between nodes that formed a DAG.

4.2   Experiment Results and Analysis

Figure 1 shows the percentage of shared keys for various pools size when changing the density of nodes in the network in a small environment of 250 by 250. As we can see from Fig. 1, the result of percentage of shared keys in the $DAGs$ becomes consistent around 50%. If the network simulated is a Distributed Sensor Network, a 50% of links between various nodes in the DSN network sharing a key is enough to guarantee full connectivity of the network. In a DSN network, nodes that do not share a key can use a neighbouring node as an indirect link as long as the link is secure. This will mean that it will take the connection between two nodes two hops rather than a direct link but both of them will be secure. However this network is an IoT network, therefore nodes that do not share a key in the routing table will be discarded. Point to Point links in RPL routing is not allowed therefore an alternative multihop secure link can not exist.

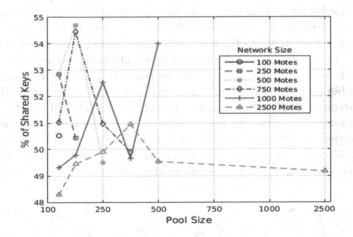

Fig. 1. Number of nodes Vs percentage of shared keys for various pools size

Figure 2 represents the ring size vs the percentage of shared keys in the DAG for various Network size. In this graph, it is very clear that the percentage of shared key $\%NSK$ is hovering around the 50%. We can also validate from Fig. 2 that the size of the ring calculation used in [4] generated a 50% shared keys between nodes in the DSN network. The percentage of $DAGs$ that contains a shared key can also be validated for IoT as 50% of the RPL routing table leaves had a common key ($\%NSK$) in the ring.

However, in a Distributed sensor network as in [4], if two nodes do not share a key they can still communicate using an indirect link (multi-hop). In an IoT network using RPL routing, multi hop alternative route is not possible. A node

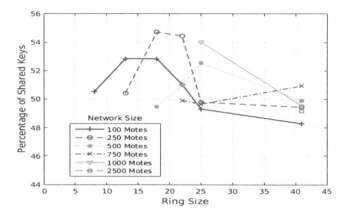

Fig. 2. Ring size Vs percentage of shared keys for various networks size

is only able to communicate with its preferred parent as per the routing table. In our experiment, if this node does not share a key with its preferred parent, then the link between those two nodes does not exist. Therefore the node will not be in the routing table and any sub leaves will also be discarded. Figure 3 show a simulation example of a 100 nodes network and how the routing table for a small subset of this network appear when simulated in the context of the Distributed Sensor Networks versus in the context of the Internet of Things. From this figure we can conclude that many nodes will be discarded if we use the key pre-distribution algorithm in its current form. This will result in an IoT network a lot smaller than the one we started with. The remaining nodes that were discarded, if the algorithm left as it is, will have to start the process of randomly selecting a new key ring and identifier ring. Nodes in the routing table will then check again whether all leaves in the routing table share a key.

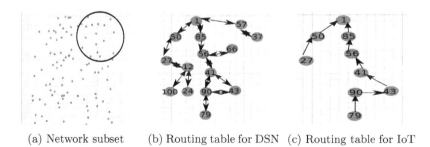

(a) Network subset   (b) Routing table for DSN   (c) Routing table for IoT

Fig. 3. Comparison of routing table for a snippets from a simulation of 100 nodes in the context of DSN Vs. IoT

4.3   Larger Key Rings

Having a small ring size for a considerably large network is a characteristic of the key pre-distribution algorithm in [4]. However and as shown in Table 2, the rings size used for previous experiment did not achieve full connectivity of the network. One alternative that we thought is essential to investigate is the size of the ring. Table 2 below show how we experimented with the ring size, modifying it until we reached 100% connectivity of the network.

Table 2. Simulation experiments over various rings size

Original values			Experiment														
			1		2		3		4		5		6				
N	RS	SK %	RS	SK %	RS	SK %	RS	SK %	RS	SK %	RS	SK %	RS	SK %			
100	8	50.52	18	84.16	22	100											
250	13	50.43	30	98.18	36	100											
500	18	57.14	30	83.17	45	99.07	48	100									
750	22	49.47	30	71.95	45	92.87	60	99.40	63	100							
1,000	25	57.14	30	63.44	45	89.28	60	97.32	75	99.53	77	100					
2,500	41	48.19			45	59.37	60	92.46	75	97.11	100	99.64	104	100			

Figure 4 show a comparison of rings size when the key pre-distribution algorithm is used in distributed Sensors network and in RPL over IoT network for various network sizes. It is very clear that the size of the ring that achieves a full network connectivity in [4] does not apply to the Internet of Things network when using RPL. To achieve full connectivity of the network, a ring size of 77 key/identifier is needed for a pool size of 1000 in comparison of a ring size of 25 key/identifier for the same pool. This is a big difference that will have a large impact on the network performance. Figure 5 show the rings size needed for various network sizes to achieve a guaranteed full connectivity between all nodes within the RPL routing table.

As we can see from Table 2 above, 104 keys were needed in the key ring to achieve a 100% guaranteed connectivity in the RPL routing table in comparison with only 41 keys in a ring needed for DSN networks . We have used 64 bits key and 32 bits identifier. This will mean that key ring and identifier ring will take up around 1.38 kb of memory storage in each node. In this experiment, we have also used Zolertia node Z1 which features a powerful a 16-bit RISC CPU, 16 MHz clock speed, 8 KB RAM and a 92 KB Flash memory. This means that at least 90 kB of Flash memory is still free to use for operating system and other applications.

However, the original plan was to use as in [4] a pool of 100,000. A simple calculation can give us an estimation of 4,600 keys and identifiers in each ring in order to guarantee connectivity in the network using RPL protocol. Ring size of 4,600 keys and identifiers will take up around 54 kb of memory storage in

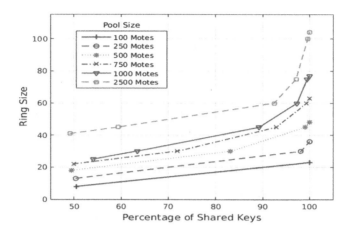

Fig. 4. Various rings size to achieve 100% of shared keys for different Pool size

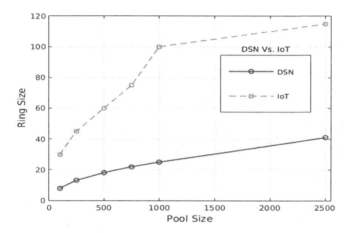

Fig. 5. Rings size in DSN Vs. rings size in IoT for various Pool size for 100% connectivity

each node. That is more than half of the memory present for the Zolertia node (Zolertia [18] has the largest amount of memory in Contiki. TMote sky node [19] is widely used and it has only 48 kb of memory which is not enough if using 4,600 keys and identifiers in each ring).

Computation overhead is another aspect that needs to be looked at. Comparing two identifiers rings will require a processing power that is very scarce. When running the same experiment using 4,600 and 104 keys in a ring, we note that during comparison of the key ring between two nodes, nodes processing power were around 87% used for 23 s. We can conclude that for a larger key ring size, nodes will not be able to cope with the computation power required and this will add a huge overhead on the network performance and the routing table establishment.

5 Conclusion and Future Work

In this paper, we investigated the performance of the key pre-distribution algorithm for distributed sensor networks on the IoT devices. We experimented with the variables and simulated small scale networks of 100 nodes to large scales network of 2500 nodes. Up until this point, we believe we have proved that the key pre-distribution algorithm achieve the 50% probability of the nodes to have a shared key, however it does not guarantee a full connectivity of the network when used in the context of the IoT. The use of RPL protocol in IoT gives a 0.45 probability of leaves in the RPL table with a shared key, which means that not all the network is able to communicate as the RPL only uses leaves that are in the routing table.

The next step in this research will be to explore alternatives solutions to secure leaves in the RPL routing table that do not share a key. In the coming few months, we will be developing a new Objective function metric.

The Objective Function uses several routing metrics to form the DODAG based on some algorithm or calculation formulas. Metrics are carried in DAG metric containers embedded in the DIO messages. The DAG metric containers at the moment are divided into two categories, node metrics and link metrics. In node metrics, nodes exchange information metrics about node state, node energy and hop count. in Link metric, nodes exchange link related information such as throughput, latency and link reliability.

We propose to add Shared Identifier Secure Link Objective Function (SISLOF) to RPL objective function metrics. SISLOF objective function will be used to quantify the shared key discovery (node metric) between two nodes that can form a direct link (neighbouring node) using a Boolean value, of 0 or 1, where 0 indicates that the two nodes do not share a common identifier and 1 indicates that the two nodes do share one or more common identifier. Further to this, the SISLOF will compute other link metrics in order to determine the suitability of the link if two links exist both with a shared key, in term of ETX and node rank.

By doing this, we ensure that any node that joins the routing table can communicate securely as only the nodes that fulfil the requirement of the SISLOF will be able to join the RPL DODAG.

References

1. Zhao, K., Ge, L.: A survey on the internet of things security. In: 9th International Conference on Computational Intelligence and Security (CIS), Leshan, pp. 663–667 (2013). doi:10.1109/CIS.2013.145
2. Tan, L., Wang, N.: Future internet: the internet of things. In: 3rd International Conference on Advanced Computer Theory and Engineering (ICACTE), Chengdu, pp. V5-376–V5-380 (2010). doi:10.1109/ICACTE.2010.5579543
3. Gan, G., Lu, Z., Jiang, J.: Internet of things security analysis. In: International Conference on Internet Technology, Applications (iTAP), Wuhan, pp. 1–4 (2011). doi:10.1109/ITAP.2011.6006307

4. Eschenauer, L., Gligor, V.D.: A key-management scheme for distributed sensor networks. In: Atluri, V. (ed.) Proceedings of the 9th ACM Conference on Computer, Communications Security (CCS 2002), pp. 41–47. ACM, New York (2011). doi:10.1145/586110.586117

5. Shelby, Z., Bormann, C.: 6LoWPAN: The Wireless Embedded Internet - Part 1: Why 6LoWPAN?, EE Times (2011). http://www.eetimes.com/document.asp?docid=1278794

6. IEEE Computer Society, 802.15.4 - Low Rate Wireless Personal Area Networks (LR-WPANs), IEEE standard for local and metropolitan area networks, IEEE, USA (2011)

7. Internet of Things, Strategic Research Roadmap; European Commission - Information Society and Media DG, European Commission, Brussels, Belgium (2009)

8. Brandt, A., Hui, J., Kelsey, R., Levis, P., Pister, K., Struik, R., Vasseur, JP., Alexander, R.: RPL: IPv6 Routing Protocol for Low-Power and Lossy Networks, In: Winter, T., Thubert, P., (eds.) IETF draft (2012). https://tools.ietf.org/html/rfc6550

9. Taso, T., Alexander, R., Dohler, M., Daza, V., Lozana, A., Richardson, M. (eds.) A Security Threat Analysis for the Routing Protocol for Low-Power and Lossy Networks (RPLs) RFC 7416, IETF trust (2015). https://tools.ietf.org/html/rfc7416

10. Carman, D.W., Kruus, P.S., Matt, B.J.: Constraints and Approaches for Distributed Sensor Network Security, NAI Labs Technical Report, 1 September 2000

11. Neuman, C., Yu, T., Hartman, S., Raeburn, K.: RFC 4129: The Kerberos Network Authentication Service (2005)

12. Noack, M.: Optimization of Two-way Authentication Protocol in Internet of Things, Master Thesis, University of Zurich, Communication Systems Group, Department of Informatics, Zurich, Switzerland (2014)

13. Porambage, P., Kumar, P., Gurtov, A., Ylianttila, M., Harjula, E.: Certificate based keying scheme for DTLS secured IoT draft-pporamba-dtls-certkey-00, IETF, June 2013

14. Contiki Operating system. http://contiki-os.org

15. Ostrelind, F.: A sensor Network Simulator for the Contiki OS, February 2006. http://soda.swedish-ict.se/2296/1/SICS-T-2006-05-SE.pdf

16. Swedberg, C.: University Caters to Students Seeks Efficiencies Through Beacons, IoT Journal, September 2016. http://www.iotjournal.com/articles/view?14936

17. IP Services, Birkbeck University of London, 23 August 2016. http://www.bbk.ac.uk/its/services/kpis/wifi-usage

18. Zolertia Low power wireless module for IoT and WSN. http://zolertia.io/z1

19. Moore, S.: Tmote Sky, August 2013. http://wirelesssensornetworks.weebly.com/1/post/2013/08/tmote-sky.html

Formulating A Global Identifier Based on Actor Relationship for the Internet of Things

Ausama Majeed[(⊠)] and Adil Al-Yasiri

School of Computing, Science, and Engineering,
University of Salford, Manchester, UK
a.a.majeed@edu.salford.ac.uk,
a.al-yasiri@salford.ac.uk

Abstract. The Internet of Things (IoT) promising a new generation of services been offered to a human being through a world of interconnected objects (called "things") that may use different communication technologies. Objects, in IoT, are seamlessly connected on its owner/user behalf. To offer services, the service providers need to truly identify the effective actor/user rather than the communicated devices. Currently, users have relationships with multiple objects that can also be used to determine their user. These relationships between actors are changeable or may even vanish; however, they are important to distinguish the actual requester of the service. Hence, it is important to consider them when identifying the effective actor of the communicated object. This paper models these relationships, representing them in a general form, and proposes a new semantic identifier format that allows service providers to identify the service requester identity across domains based on those relationships.

Keywords: IoT · Identity · Identifier · Actor relationship

1 Introduction

The Internet of Things (IoT) represents a technological revolution in the communication and computing fields. The core idea of IoT can be summarised in the sentence "a worldwide network of interconnected entities" [1]. All IoT entities (people, applications/ services, and devices) have to be communicated over the Internet. Entities can communicate with each other, either directly or indirectly, oblivious to the underline technology being used. The ultimate goal of these communicated entities is to offer a better service for the human beings. They vary regarding technical specifications, computing and communication capabilities, and deployment fields. Moreover, entities have to be uniquely identified to facilitate entities distinguishing.

To manage and control interaction with those entities, every network domain employs a suitable Identity Management (IdM) system [2]. IdM is considered the cornerstone of the identity lifecycle. The identity is used to describe an entity within a specific context based on the characteristics of this entity, which can be attributed to the entity distinctly in that context. Theoretically, an entity can have several different

© ICST Institute for Computer Sciences, Social Informatics and Telecommunications Engineering 2017
N. Mitton et al. (Eds.): InterIoT 2016/SaSeIot 2016, LNICST 190, pp. 79–91, 2017.
DOI: 10.1007/978-3-319-52727-7_10

identity attributes [3–5]. IdM processes encompass the management of the entity identities and their authentication, authorization, roles, and privileges and permissions within or across system and enterprise boundaries [6]. IdMs aim to assure that the service provider (SP) will offer services to a trusted requester based on a pre-established trust relationship with the identity provider IdP to increase enterprises security and productivity.

From a technical point of view, IoT encompasses an enormous amount of connected devices and objects. These devices and objects are interconnected on behalf of other IoT entities (interested parties). For instances, people interact with mobile phones (or tablets), companies' inventory systems interact with RFID (Radio Frequency ID) readers to monitor their assets, insurance companies use telematics devices to monitor the young drivers' behaviour, etc. The interaction requires at least a relationship between two entities. These relationships might not always be static in nature; it could be dynamically established and after a period will be changed or even vanish. One can think of scenarios of how to interact with freely available devices (or things in general) to request services. For example, the interaction between an active RFID tag, which is attached to a rented car, and an electronic toll system reader to pay a parking charge, or many similar scenarios. This means that IoT will change the current ways of interaction with entities from "owner" and "subscriber" to much broader ways such as interact with free devices as discussed in [7–9]. However, all IoT entities have to be uniquely identified, hence identifying such relationships has a significant role to the success of the IoT. This is because there are many to many (m:n) interactions between devices in the IoT environment [9] which are communicated on behalf of other entities. The current communications between these IoT things lack the means to identify the relationships. Thus, there is a need for a new identifier format that could lead to identifying the effective entity through its relationship with the IoT communicated device(s). This paper presents an identifier that could be used for global identification of IoT entities that takes into consideration such relationships.

The rest of the paper is organised as follows: Sect. 2 reviews the state of the art related to IoT identification; Sect. 3 discusses IoT actors, identify the relationships between them and finally modelling the relationships. These relationships are represented in Global Actor Relationship Identifier format in Sect. 4, which also includes an example of a typical identifier. Section 5 evaluates the new identifier by comparing the current identifier proposals with the one proposed in this work. Section 6 concludes the paper with references at the end.

2 Related Work

There are several proposals to develop an identifier to use in the IoT environment. These can be summarised as follows.

Liu et al. [10] proposed an identifier format used to control the sensor nodes remotely in the IoT. They focused on object identification without considering the owner (or user) identity of that device, nor its relationship with an enterprise (or a real person). Their identifier was composed of a domain identifier, device type and the device identifier using a URL style using 64-bits to formulate their identifier using the format "dev://domain-series/devtype/legacy-name".

Mahalle et al. [7, 11] stated that an entity's identification could be defined by using a collection of three parameters which are: *type*, *identifier*, and *namespace* in which that identifier assigned to the entity. However, the proposal ignores an important parameter which is the Internet connectivity characteristic of the entity. This is because they built their work on the assumption that all entities with computing capabilities. That means their identification ignores a large community of tiny and low capability objects, which fill the IoT environment. Accordingly, they proposed objects and resources identifier format for IoT, which is composed of a set of permanent or temporary attributes that represent each end-point identification. Object mobility was considered through using a global namespace and local namespace parameters. However, user representation is missing again and in turn, the relationship between the user and the object is missing. The research is limited to the internet protocol (IP) connected devices without considering other communication technologies that use intermediary devices to connect to the Internet.

Batalla and Krawiec [12] proposed an object/service identifier, which was composed of a chain of all the names, separated by a dot starting from the root; but again it lacked a mention of the users. This identifier was proposed for sensory environments and focused on controlling fixed devices remotely such as controlling a smart home appliance. For example, to communicate with a light on in the first room, a control message could be send using the format (.*floor001.room0001.lightctr*) followed by the control command.

Van Thuan and Butkus [13] proposed an identifier format composed of a set of identities based on URL format. It contained IdP identifier, domain identifier, device identifier, and a user identifier as follows:

idpID	domIDPart	devIDPart	userIDPart

idp.google.com /item.ntnu.no/phone_101 /namesurn

This identifier is used to identify the owner of the devices, and the researchers assumed that both of them were registered within the same IdP. Moreover, they only considered devices with computing resources and neglected other devices with low computing capabilities. Again, the research was limited to connected devices with the Internet Protocol and ignored other communication technologies.

Zdravkova [14] proposed an identifier format for the IoT, which was composed of the following parameters: device type, domain identifier, user identifier, and a device identifier as follow: "dtype|gIoTnt|unidomID|unidevID|uniuID". The identifier used a device type to specify the type of entity that is identified by this identifier; this entity could be a person or device. However, the relationship between user and device was missing again. The domain identifier was used for both the user and the device without considering that they could be different.

As shown from this discussion, a new identifier is required to meet two requirements: firstly, to identify the effective entity that initiated the communication (e.g. a user) which may not be the entity that is connected to the Internet, and secondly to allow dynamic relationships between such entities over the IoT.

3 Actors and Actor Relationships in the IoT

3.1 Actors in IoT

As explained above, the communicated devices are intent to interact with other devices to offer a service to other interested parties. All of them represent actors in the IoT environment. In our research, we use the *actor* concept of the IoT to refer to widely used terms with different meanings. A number of terms have been utilised in the literature with no clear definitions of these terms. They are entity, object, thing and actor, which are depicted in Fig. 1. Their meaning is often mixed up and confused by the reader. Therefore, we define them as follows:

- *Entity:* A general term used to describe any identified component in the IoT environment, which has an identity and a set of attributes that describe it. Entities represent a person, a car, a place, an organisation, an application or more that tend to communicate with other entities to send or receive information or control messages.
- *Object:* Any entity that embeds (or attached to) a communication device. The communication device allows entities to communicate with each other and before accessing the Internet. It may use various communication technologies such as Radio Frequency (RF), Near Field Communication (NFC), BlueTooth BT, Wireless Fidelity (WiFi), etc. A person who interacts with a wearable Fitbit or a PC that is not connected to the Internet are examples of the IoT's object.
- *Thing:* An object, which has Internet connectivity. Therefore, the object becomes an active participant in the information network, i.e. a thing, as it is accessible by the Internet and able to share its data with interested parties. The terms "smart object" and "smart thing" are denoting to the same meaning of "thing" [15, 16].
- *Actor:* Represents any entity, object or thing from the IoT environment that interacts with each other to communicate with a (possibly remote) real other object or thing to achieve a goal. The goal could be to monitor, move, manipulate that object, or set/get some interesting information [17, 18].

From the above definitions, all "things" in the IoT are instances of 'entity', but not all entities can become things. For example, a hospital wheelchair, which has a unique identifier to distinguish it from others is an entity in the IoT. To allow this wheelchair become part of the IoT as a thing, it requires having Internet connectivity. By attaching a suitable communication device to the wheelchair, it will be able to communicate within its area using a suitable technology. In the case of using a technology that does not have *Internet Connectivity (i.e. IP stack)* such as BT, it is still able to communicate within its domain. In such a case, it will be denoted as an "object". An additional device is used to act as an Internet gateway to connect the wheelchair as an object to the Internet. Next, this object (i.e. the wheelchair with the communication device) has to be accessible by the Internet to call it a "thing" in IoT. By linking it to a patient's smartphone, the wheelchair becomes a thing in the IoT and now can send or receive data through the information network.

From the above scenario, it is clear that there are two relationships: the first relationship is between the wheelchair and the communication device, while the second one is between the communication device and the smartphone being used to access the Internet. These relationships represent interactions between different actors and aim to allow the entity to become a thing in the IoT. Therefore, the wheelchair, communication device, and the smartphone, as an Internet gateway, are represented actors in IoT that have different relationships with each other.

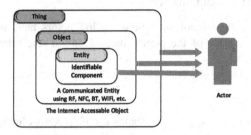

Fig. 1. Entity, object, thing, and actor demonstration

3.2   Relationship Types Between Actors

The IoT things collaborate/interact with each other to serve interested parties that could be a user, a company, etc. Offering the right service requires identifying the actor/user correctly. This interaction could be found between people and their related devices or things, between different communicated devices, between people and applications/ services, or between devices and applications/services. Identifying these relationships has a bearing on truly identifying the actual actor of the communicating device(s), as it will lead to offering the right service to a true requester.

Relationships between actors in IoT may be classified into three types as follows:

1. *Permanent relationship:* In this relationship type, objects are collaborated to offer services to only one Actor. Such relationship could be found with patient monitoring devices, personal equipment, etc.
2. *Semi-Permanent relationship:* Objects collaborate to offer services to several actors but one at a time. The relationships have to be pre-established with the actors. The objects need to offer a suitable service for each actor. The automated teller machines and company's assets are examples of this relationship.
3. *Free relationship:* In this case, the objects are collaborated to offer services to any interested actor. No relationship needs to be established with the objects. Using an airport's public personal computer or stores self-check out machines are examples of this relationship.

In the first type of relationship, i.e. a permanent relationship, both of relationship participants have to be able to identify the other party. In other words, each participant has to be linked to the other by precisely registered it with the IdPs. For instance, a patient medical record with a medical centre would be able to attribute a health monitoring device that is attached to the patient and vice versa. Similarly, in the second relationship type, a group of actors has a relationship with a participant. Each participant would be able to attribute the second participant identity and vice versa. However, the free relationship type would not help to identify the relationship participants. This is because it is established without updating the participants' record. Therefore, it could not be used to attribute the identity of the participants.

3.3   Modelling Actor Relationships

As discussed above, the relationships between IoT actors have an essential role to attribute the effective actor of the communicated one. These relationships could be represented as follows.

3.3.1   Definitions

Definition 1 IoT Actor. Let A_{IoT} represents the set of all Actors in the IoT environment.

$$A_{IoT} = \{a_1, a_2, \ldots, a_n\} \tag{1}$$

Where,

$$\forall a_l \in A_{IoT}, a_l = Person\,|Device\,|Application\,|\,Service;$$
$$l = 1, 2, \ldots, n; n = total\ number\ of\ things.$$

That Actor (a_l) could be a person, a device, an application or a service that interacts with other objects to perform a required task.

Definition 2 Primary Actor. An Actor could be classified into *Primary* or *Secondary* according to the purpose of the communication in IoT. A *Primary Actor* (A_P) represents a subset of A_{IoT} that tend to initiate or consume services with no Internet connectivity. A_P could be defined as follows:

$$A_P \subset A_{IoT} \tag{2}$$

Where,

$$\forall a_i \in A_P, a_i = entity\,|\,object; i = 1, 2, \ldots, m;$$
$$m = total\ number\ of\ primary\ actors$$

Definition 3 Secondary Actor. A *Secondary Actor* (A_S) represents a subset of A_{IoT} composed of communication objects (co) being used by an actor (a_i) to perform a required task. Members of A_S could be either object or thing, such as a tag reader, an IoT gateway, a mobile device, a PC, etc.

$$A_S \subset A_{IoT} \tag{3}$$

Where,

$$\forall co_j \in A_S, co_j = object \,|\, thing; j = 1, 2, \ldots, p;$$
$$p = total \; number \; of \; secondary \; actors$$

3.3.2 Actor Relationship

A *communication object* (co) can be categorised according to its *Internet Connectivity* (IC) into two types of A_S. The first type is *Active Object* (O_A), which is a (co) with the ability to connect to the Internet (implements the Internet Protocol IP stack), such as a smartphone. The second type is *Passive Object* (O_P), which is a (co) that does not have Internet connectivity and relies on another O_A member to access the Internet. Typical examples of such objects are a tag (e.g. RFID, BT, or NFC), a body sensor node, application, etc. These O_A and O_P could be defined as follows:

$$O_A = \{co_m : co_m \in A_S \land co_m \text{ have the IP stack}\} \tag{4}$$

$$O_P = \{co_n : co_n \in A_S \land co_n \text{ does not have the IP stack}\} \tag{5}$$

The *Internet Connectivity* (IC) of A_S members could be defined based on (4) and (5) as follows:

$$IC(co_k) = \begin{cases} Active, & co_k \in O_A \\ Passive, & co_k \in O_P \end{cases} \tag{6}$$

Where,

$$\forall co_k \in A_S; k = 1, 2, \ldots, q$$

To identify the active actor of any communicated object, in the IoT, the interaction between them is required to be explicitly represented using a relationship. Let an actor relationship, denoted by "*AR*", represents an interaction of two IoT Actors. The first actor is $(a_i \in A_P)$ that interacts with the second actor $(co_j \in A_S)$ to allow (a_i) fulfils a required task. The "*AR*" could be defined as follows:

$$\forall a_i \in A_P, \exists co_j \in A_S$$
$$AR_{i,j} = \text{Uses } (a_i, co_j) \tag{7}$$

The $IC(co_j)$ type plays an important role to access the Internet, as previously discussed. Depending on the $IC(co_j)$ we have two cases:

- The *first one* is where the $IC(co_j)$ type is *active*; this means the (co_j) is able to link (a_i) to the Internet directly. Therefore, $AR_{i,j}$, as defined in (7), is able to link (a_i) to the Internet to become part of IoT environment.
- The *second case* is where the $IC(co_j)$ is *passive*, which means the (co_j) is unable to link (a_i) to the Internet directly. Therefore, (co_j) still requires to interact with another *secondary actor*, e.g. $(co_r \in A_s)$, to access the Internet. If such a relationship exists between $(co_j$ and $co_r)$ and $IC(co_r)$ is *active*, thus the (a_i) can link to the Internet through a transitive relationship between $(a_i$ and $co_r)$. Then, the *Transitive Actor Relationship* (TR) will show the existence of a relationship between $(a_i$ and $co_r)$, i.e. $(AR_{i,r})$, or not.

Let us assume there exist a $(co_r : co_r \in O_A)$, the $(AR_{j,r})$ relationship between $(co_j \in O_P)$ and (co_r) could be defined following the AR relationship in (7) as follows:

$$\text{Let } co_j \in O_P, co_r \in O_A$$
$$Uses(co_j, co_r) = AR_{j,r} \tag{8}$$

The relationship in (8) represents the interaction between a pair of secondary actors where one belongs to O_P and the other belongs to O_A.

We can now define a *general actor relationship* for the IoT that is composed of n Actors using the relationships defined in (6), (7) and (8) as follows:

$$\text{Let } n = \text{the number of actors}, n > 1$$
$$\forall a_i \in A_{IoT}, 1 \leq i \leq n-1$$
$$AR_{i,i+1} = \begin{cases} Uses(a_i, a_{i+1}), & n = 2, a_{i+1} \in O_A \\ 0, & n = 2, a_{i+1} \in O_P \\ Uses(a_i, AR_{i+1,i+2}), & \text{Otherwise} \end{cases} \tag{9}$$

4 Global Actor Relationship Identifier Format

Identity means something that describes an "entity" accurately to distinguish it from other entities in a domain. An *identifier* is a way that represents this "entity" by using a series of numbers, characters, or a combination of them, which is meaningful in a specific domain (namespace). The *namespace* represents the application area of the "entity" identifier and can be used to distinguish it from others. The Identity Provider system (*IdP*) is responsible for issuing, assigning, and managing the entity's identifier within a namespace.

Representing the identity of an "actor" in IoT requires an identifier that contains sufficient information to identify it at any visited domain across its registration one. As discussed in Sect. 2, the identity parameters proposed by Mahalle et al., are insufficient to identify neither tiny actors nor actors across their namespace (domain). To resolve this limitation, the identity of an actor is extended to four parameters instead of three by considering the actor's Internet connectivity. In addition to minor modification of *namespace* parameter to be *IdP* name to facilitate the identity verification process across domains. A new identifier format is developed based on our identity parameters to build the actor identity for the IoT. These parameters are *Type, Internet Connectivity, Identifier* and *identity provider* of the domain that assigned this identifier to the actor. Although it seems obvious, it is important to note that actor with active Internet connectivity can only be of a device actor type as it represents the communication device. Thus, the Identity of an Actor is represented as follows:

$$\forall\, a_l \in A_{IoT}$$
$$Identity(a_l) = \{T(a_l), IC(a_l), Id(a_l), IdP(a_l)\} \tag{10}$$

Where,

$T(a_l)$ Represents the **actor's type**, as defined in (1);
$IC(a_l)$ Represents the **actor's ability to access the Internet**, as defined in (5);
$Id(a_l)$ Represents the **identifier** that is assigned to (a_l) by the IdP;
$IdP(a_l)$ Represents **the domain's identity provider** in which the identifier is assigned to (a_l);

To formulate a *Global Actor Relationship Identifier* (*GARI*) we have to re-represent the general actor relationship, which is defined in (9), in a way that is able to show the actor identity parameters defined in (10). Thus, we propose the following (*GARI*) format that is composed of three main parts as follows:

- *Actors_Relation_Specifier,* which is used to specify the characteristics of the relationship participants. These are firstly, the type of (a_i) as it defined in (1). Secondly, $IC(a_j)$ to determine the way of contacting (a_i). Thirdly, (TR) to specify the existence of a transitive actor relationship when $IC(a_j)$ is *passive*, as discussed in (8). Finally, the relationship type, as discussed earlier in 3.2, which will allow the *SP* to decide whether the $IdP(a_j)$ will query to verify the (a_i) identity or not.
- *Identification*(a_i), it is used to specify the identifier of (a_i) and the *IdP* (a_i) that assign this identifier.
- *Identification*(a_j), it could be represented in two forms according to the $IC(a_j)$ type in the first part. The first form is similar to the second part to represent the identification of (a_j) when the $IC(a_j)$ type is *active*. Whilst, the second form is to represent the additional actor relationship (if existent) when the $IC(a_j)$ type is *passive*.

The (*GARI*) format is defined as follow:

$$GARI = \{Actors\_Relation\_Specifier, Identification(a_i),$$
$$Identification(a_j)\} \tag{11}$$

Where,

$$a_i \in A_P \subset A_{IoT}; a_j \in A_S \subset A_{IoT};$$

$$Actors\_Relation\_Specifier = \left\{ T(a_i), IC(a_j), TR, T(AR_{i,j}) \right\} \qquad (11.1)$$

$$Identification(a_i) = \left\{ IdP(a_i) : Id(a_i) \right\} \qquad (11.2)$$

$$Identification(a_j) = \left\{ IdP(a_j) : Id(a_j) \right\} \qquad (11.3)$$

GARI contains all the required information that will facilitate identifying the effective actor by the *SP* as the end point of service request. Thus, the *SP's* confidence of offering their services to the right requester will be improved by involving more *IdPs* in the requester identification process based on the relationship type.

To illustrate the actor relationship, in *GARI*, of an entity in IoT, let us consider the wheelchair scenario, discussed earlier in Sect. 3.1 as an example. In this scenario, shown in Fig. 2, there are three actors (a primary actor and two secondary actors) and two relationships. The first relationship ($AR_{1,2}$) is between the wheelchair as a primary actor and the BT communication device attached to it. However, $AR_{1,2}$ is unable to access the Internet as $IC(a_2)$ is *passive*. Thus, the second relationship is needed to link the wheelchair to the Internet. The second relationship ($AR_{2,3}$) is between the BT device and the smartphone with WiFi technology to access the Internet. Although the $IC(a_2)$ is *passive*, it is obvious that the *TR* does not exist between (a_1) and (a_3).

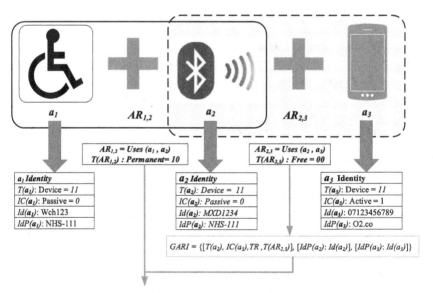

Fig. 2. An example of *GARI* composing

To allow the wheelchair to be uniquely identified in the IoT, we have to compose a *GARI* identifier based on these relationships.

As shown in Fig. 2, the receiver of the *GARI* message can recognize that the effective actor of this communication is a *passive* device (the 0 value in *IC* field) and the two relationships between the three actors. Moreover, the *NHS-111* is the only *IdP* that could be used to identify the effective actor because of its permanent relationship type and inexistence of a transitive relationship to use the $IdP(a_3)$. This way, *GARI* helps the receiver to identify the effective actor.

5 Evaluation

Identifying the effective actor of a communicated device across domains in an open environment like IoT is still an issue facing *SPs*. This is because the nomadic nature of the IoT entities that can freely join and leave different *SPs* to get their services. To solve this problem, *SPs* need a new identification method that can seamlessly interoperate with external *IdPs* based on dynamically establishing trust relationships to identify the actor's identity. This method might improve the *SPs* interoperability as the IoT is a huge community of entities and identifying them requires more dynamic and scalable method. This method requires a special identifier format that contains sufficient information, which is what we focused on in this paper. However, this is a work in progress, and more work is underway to develop an identification method and protocol before the format is thoroughly tested. In this section, we evaluate the proposed format based on its perceived benefits in comparison to other identifiers.

The comparison between existing identifier proposals and *GARI* is presented in Table 1. The table shows that almost all of the proposals encompass the *device identifier* and the *IdP (or domain namespace)* information. However, all existing proposals lack any information related to the *user type* of the communicated device. In addition, none has considered the *user-device relationships,* which we believe to be essential in identifying the effective actors. By specifying these relationships in *GARI*, *SPs* will be able to identify the *IdPs* to be used in the identification of the effective actor, based on the *relationship type* and the *transitive actor relationship* existence. Moreover, all existing methods ignored *Internet Connectivity* of the entities, assuming all devices able to access the Internet. Thus, existing identifiers are unable to identify passive objects globally in comparison with *GARI*.

To sum up, existing proposals fail to distinguish between primary and secondary actors. In other words, it will not be possible for connected parties to make a distinction between those who make a connection on behalf of others. In comparison, GARI makes it possible to use relationships between actors and cross-domain information to identify such entities.

Table 1. State of the art of identifiers comparison

Criteria	Identifier proposals					
	Liu et al.	Batalla et al.	Mahalle et al.	Thuan et al.	Zdravkova	GARI
User type						✓
Device type	✓			✓	✓	✓
User-device relationship						✓
User identifier			✓	✓	✓	✓
User domain/IdP			✓		✓	✓
Device identifier	✓	✓	✓	✓	✓	✓
Device domain/IdP	✓	✓	✓	✓	✓	✓
Mobility/cross-domain support			✓	✓	✓	✓
Internet connectivity						✓
Ability to identifies passive objects						✓

6 Conclusion

The IoT is a technology revolution that will change the relationships between inter-connected entities. Identifying these relationships has a direct impact on the identification of the effective actor of the communicated object. The Internet connectivity of the communication object leads identifying its ways to access the Internet as it might require establishing an additional relationship when the object is passive. This will allow a broad range of tiny and passive objects to be part of the IoT and recognise them globally by following these relationships. Although previous work has used multiple parameters to identify these entities, such parameters are insufficient to fully describe how entities collaborate to establish a connection to the Internet. In this work, we argued that the identity of entities in IoT could be sufficiently established based on the existence of four parameters: type, Internet connectivity, identifier and the Idp. Therefore, to identify the entities globally in IoT we need to represent these relationships and all other required information in a semantic identifier format. The relationships in the IoT are defined and modelled in this research and then represented in a new identifier format (called GARI), to solve this issue. Further work is underway to develop a new identification method and a protocol that will be used to verify the identity of the effective actor of communicated devices across-domains.

References

1. Roman, R., Zhou, J., Lopez, J.: On the features and challenges of security and privacy in distributed internet of things. Comput. Netw. 57(10), 2266–2279 (2013)
2. Fongen, A.: Identity management and integrity protection in the Internet of Things. In: 3rd International Conference on Emerging Security Technologies, pp. 111–114, IEEE Press (2012)

3. Alpár, G., Hoepman, J.-H., Siljee, J.: The Identity Crisis. Security, Privacy and Usability Issues in Identity Management (2011). arXiv Preprint arXiv1101.0427

4. Angin, P., Bhargava, B., Ranchal, R., Singh, N., Linderman, M., Othmane, L.B, Lilien, L.: An entity-centric approach for privacy and identity management in cloud computing. In: 29th IEEE Symposium on Reliable Distributed Systems, pp. 177–183. IEEE Press, New Delhi (2010)

5. Jøsang, A, Golbeck, J.: Challenges for robust trust and reputation systems. In: Proceedings of the 5th International Workshop on Security and Trust Management (SMT 2009), Saint Malo (2009)

6. Yeluri, R., Castro-Leon, E.: Identity management and control for clouds. In: Building the Infrastructure for Cloud Security, pp. 141–159. Apress (2014)

7. Mahalle, P.N., Railkar, P.N.: Identity Management for Internet of Things. River Publishers, Denmark (2015)

8. Gartner: The Identity of Things for the Internet of Things - (G00270277) (2015)

9. Forgerock: Whitepaper: The Identity of Things (IDoT): Access Management (IAM) Reference Architecture for The Internet of Things (IoT) (2015)

10. Liu, C.H., Yang, B., Liu, T.: Efficient naming, addressing and profile services in Internet-of-Things sensory environments. Ad Hoc Netw. **18**, 85–101 (2014)

11. Mahalle, P.N., Prasad, N.R., Prasad, R.: Novel context-aware clustering with hierarchical addressing (CCHA) for the Internet-of-Things (IoT). In: 5th International Conference on Advances in Recent Technologies in Communication and Computing (ARTCom 2013), pp. 267–274. IET, Bangalore (2013)

12. Batalla, J.M., Krawiec, P.: Conception of ID layer performance at the network level for Internet of Things. Pers. Ubiquit. Comput. **18**(2), 465–480 (2014)

13. Van Thuan, D., Butkus, P.: A user centric identity management for Internet of Things. In: International Conference on IT Convergence and Security (ICITCS), pp. 1–4. IEEE Publisher, Beijing (2014)

14. Zdravkova, V.: Identity management approach in Internet of Things. Aalborg University (2015)

15. Vujovic, V., Maksimovic, M., Kosmajac, D., Perisic, B.: Resource: a connection between Internet of Things and resource-oriented architecture. In: Proceedings of Smart SysTech 2015, European Conference on Smart Objects, Systems and Technologies, pp. 1–7. VDE Publisher, Aachen (2015)

16. Bello, O., Zeadally, S.: Intelligent device-to-device communication in the Internet of Things. IEEE Syst. J. **99**, 1–11 (2015)

17. Serbanati, A., Medaglia, C.M., Ceipidor, U.B.: Building Blocks of the Internet of Things: State of the Art and Beyond. INTECH Open Access Publisher, Rijeka (2011)

18. Bassi, A., Bauer, M., Fiedler, M., Kramp, T., Van Kranenburg, R., Lange, S., Meissner, S.: Enabling Things to Talk. Designing IoT Solutions with the IoT Architectural Reference Model, pp. 163–211. Springer, Heidelberg (2013)

Framework of Cyber Attack Attribution Based on Threat Intelligence

Li Qiang[1,2], Yang Zeming[2], Liu Baoxu[2], Jiang Zhengwei[2(✉)], and Yan Jian[1,2]

[1] University of Chinese Academy of Science,
Beijing, People's Republic of China
[2] Institute of Information Engineering, CAS,
Beijing, People's Republic of China
{liqiang7,yangzeming,liubaoxu,
jiangzhengwei,yanjian}@iie.ac.cn

Abstract. With the rapid growth of information technology, more and more devices are connected to the network. Cyber security environment has become increasingly complicated. In the face of advanced threats, such as targeted attack and advanced persistent threat, traditional security measures of accumulating security devices to protect relevant systems and networks had been proved to be an unqualified failure. Aiming at this situation, this paper proposed a framework of cyber attack attribution based on threat intelligence. At first, after surveying and analyzing related academic research and industry solutions, this paper used the local advantage model to analysis the process of cyber attack. According to the definitions of seven steps in intrusion kill chains and six phases of F2T2EA model, this model proposed a method of collecting threat intelligence data and detecting and response to cyber attacks, so as to achieve the goals of early-warning, processing detection and response and posting attribution analysis, and finally to reverse the security situation. Then, this paper designed a framework of cyber attack attribution based on threat intelligence. The framework is composed by Start of analysis, Threat intelligence and Attribution analysis. The three main parts indicated the architecture of cyber attack attribution. Finally, we tested the framework by practical case. The case study shows that the proposed framework can provide some help in attribution analysis.

Keywords: Cyber attack attribution · Framework · Threat intelligence · Intrusion kill chains · Advanced threat

1 Introduction

With the rapid development of information technology, a huge number of devices connect to the network. Information infrastructure plays key role in business and daily life. In the past, the main security measure was accumulating security devices to protect relevant systems and networks. Ignoring the influence in functions and performances, these security measures had played a certain action in protection of conventional cyber attacks. However, aiming at complex advanced threat, such as targeted attack and advanced persistent threat, the current security measures did not seem to have done as

© ICST Institute for Computer Sciences, Social Informatics and Telecommunications Engineering 2017
N. Mitton et al. (Eds.): InterIoT 2016/SaSeIot 2016, LNICST 190, pp. 92–103, 2017.
DOI: 10.1007/978-3-319-52727-7_11

much good as we hoped. An advanced threat refers to a type of threat in which threat actors actively pursue and compromise a target entity's infrastructure while maintaining anonymity [1]. Because these attackers have a certain level of expertise and sufficient resources to conduct their schemes over a long-term period, it is hard to defend and trace advanced threat. For enterprises and governments, advanced threat would lead to harm of reputation or leakage of significant information. Cyber attack attribution analysis is significant.

One definition of cyber attack attribution is "determining the identity or location of an attacker or an attacker's intermediary [2]". According to reconstructing the attack path and the depth and fineness of attack attribution, cyber attack attribution can be divided into four levels [3, 4]: (1) Attribution to the specific hosts involved in the attack, (2) Attribution to the primary controlling host, (3) Attribution to the actual human actor, (4) Attribution to an organization with the specific intent to attack. Effective cyber attack attribution can slow down the paces of attacks. Powerful capacity of attribution is a kind of deterrence [5].

There are several techniques used in cyber attack attribution analysis. Threat intelligence is one of the typical comprehensive methods which we focused on in this paper. According to Gartner definition, threat intelligence is evidence-based knowledge, including context, mechanisms, indicators, implications and actionable device, about an existing or emerging menace or hazard to asset that can be used to inform decisions regarding the subject's response to that menace or hazard [6]. Threat intelligence is based on the collection of intelligence which using open source intelligence, social media intelligence, human intelligence or intelligence in the deep and dark webs. Key mission of threat intelligence is researching and analyzing trends and technical developments in cybercrime, cyber activism and cyber espionage [7]. Threat intelligence is not negate previous security mechanisms, but integrate various security resources to achieve the goals of early-warming, process detection and response and post attribution analysis, and finally to reverse the security situation.

In this paper, we used a local advantage model to deal with cyber attack. This model proposed a method of collecting threat intelligence data and detecting and response to attacks. The goals of cyber attack attribution are early-warming, processing detection and response and posting attribution analysis, and finally reversing the security situation. In order to introduce the process and method of cyber attack attribution analysis, we designed a framework. This framework is mainly composed by the start of analysis, threat intelligence and attribution analysis. Finally, we tested the framework by practical case and got expecting effect.

The main contribution of this paper is proposing a framework for cyber attribution analysis. The framework introduces the processes and components of cyber attack attribution. We also used the designed framework of cyber attack attribution in practical case study. The result shows that the proposed framework can provide some help in cyber attack attribution.

The rest of this paper is organized as follows. The next section describes related work about cyber attack attribution in academic research and industry solutions. Section 3 discusses our research on local advantage model and framework. Section 4 presents a practical case study about cyber attack attribution. Section 5 discusses the proposed framework and practical case. Section 6 concludes this paper and points out some future research directions.

2　Related Work

2.1　Academic Research

In the research of cyber attack analysis, F2T2EA model [8] was one of the earliest theoretical models which was proposed by United States Air Force and used in intelligence identification, supervision and investigation. The six phases of F2T2EA model are Find, Fix, Track, Target, Engage and Access. During Find step, possible targets are detected and classified for further prosecution. The Fix step of dynamic targeting includes actions to determine the location of the potential target. During Track step, the target is observed and its activity and movement are monitored. During Target step, the decision is made to engage the target in some manner to create desired effects and the means to do so are selected and coordinated. In Engage step, action is taken against the target. The Assessment phase is common to both deliberate and dynamic targeting of the joint targeting cycle and examines the results of the target engagement. United States Department of Defense [9] described the F2T2EA model as the six phases of kill chains in military field, and later it extended to cyber space security.

Lockheed Martin Corporation [10] came up with the intrusion kill chains which are the basic theory of cyber attack attribution analysis. The intrusion kill chains defined seven steps of cyber attack intrusion: reconnaissance, weaponization, delivery, exploitation, installation, command and control (C2), and action on objectives. Reconnaissance means research, identification and selection of targets. Weaponization refers to coupling a remote access Trojan with an exploit into a deliverable payload, typically by means of an automated tool (weaponizer). Delivery points Transmission of the weapon to the targeted environment. Exploitation means exploitation triggers intruders' code after the weapon is delivered to victim host. Installation means installation of a remote access Trojan or backdoor on the victim system which allows the adversary to maintain persistence inside the environment. Command and Control (C2) points that compromised hosts must beacon outbound to an Internet controller server to establish a C2 channel. Actions on Objectives mean that intruders can take actions to achieve their original objectives after progressing through the first six phases. Those kill chains phases can describe the whole systematic process to target and engage an adversary to create desired effects. The use of threat intelligence is a key component. The indicator is the fundamental element of intelligence in this model.

Sergio Catagirone [11] proposed a diamond model expected to add the cost of cyber attack and decrease the cost of defender. Diamond model provides a method to integrate the intelligence for analysis platform and make correlation, classification and forecast based on activities of attackers. The basic element of diamond model is event. Each event composed of four core features: adversary, capability, infrastructure and victim. These features are edge-connected representing their underlying relationships and arranged in the shape of a diamond. These elements, the event, thread, and group all contribute to a foundational and comprehensive model of intrusion activity built around analytic processes.

Thomas Rid [12] proposed a Q model designed to explain, guide, and improve the attribution. The paper holds the opinion that matching an offender to an offence is an exercise in minimizing uncertainty on three levels: tactically, attribution is an art as well as a science; operationally, attribution is a nuanced process not a black-and-white problem; and strategically, attribution is a function of what is at stake politically. Successful attribution requires a range of skills on all levels, careful management, time, leadership, stress-testing, prudent communication, and recognizing limitations and challenges.

The above models and methods mostly were proposed for specific requirements in specific scenarios, so there are some differences in research fields and focuses. This paper discussed the framework of cyber attack attribution based on threat intelligence. The discussed models and methods can provide some references in idea and research methods, especially F2T2EA model and intrusion kill chains.

2.2   Industry Solutions

In the industry of cyber security, there are several solutions aimed at cyber attack. Owning over 300 million users and over 250000 corporate clients worldwide, Kaspersky Lab [13] has powerful malware analysis ability which has over more than 1000 research and development experts, especially the Global Research and Analysis Team (GReAT) established in 2008. GReAT is an elite group of recognized cyber security experts located around the globe and bring local expertise and threat intelligence to monitor the world threat landscape. Till now, GReAT had discovered many sophisticated threats and release relevant APT intelligence reports, like Duqu, Flame, Gauss, Red October, etc [14].

FireEye [15] is a publicly listed us network security company which founded in 2004. The FireEye Intelligence Center provides access to strategic intelligence, analysis tools, intelligence sharing capabilities, and institutional knowledge based on over 10 years of FireEye and Mandiant experience detecting, responding to and tracking advanced threats. FireEye's intelligence databases can provide real-time, actionable intelligence analytical ability which is a patented 115+ million node graph-based engine with 340 million defined relationships, 600 terabytes of storage and over 500+ million reviewed network streams. Till now, FireEye has proposed several influential APT analysis reports, like APT1, APT28, APT30, etc [16].

Dell SecureWorks [17] proposed the security integration method from core asset to service and business value. They develop the counter threat platform which is at the core of intelligence-driven information security solutions. The counter threat platform [18] can analyze more than 160 billion network events to discover potential threats, deliver countermeasures and generate intelligence and valuable context regarding the intentions and actions of adversaries.

IBM X-Force Research and Development [19] is one of the most renowned commercial security research and development teams in the world. These security professionals monitor and analyze security issues from a variety of sources, including its database of more than 96,000 computer security vulnerabilities, its global web crawler can collect and detect over 25 B catalogued web pages and URLS, and millions of malware samples daily.

The above industry solutions are is focusing on the deployment and implement of business. They mostly used threat intelligence as an effective technology in malware analysis and cyber attack detection and attribution. In view of business secrets, the introduction of industry solutions excludes detailed information about framework and content, but it can provide some ideas and references, especially the technical solution and implement.

3 Our Research

According to the reference of related work and the actual situation, we used the local advantage model [20] to make full use of threat intelligence data from kinds of self-building security platforms and external channels to achieve the goals of early-warming, process detection and response and post attribution analysis. We also designed a framework of cyber attack attribution to solve the hardship in cyber attack analysis. Detail introductions are shown as follows.

3.1 Local Advantage Model

According to the definitions of seven steps in kill chains and six phases of F2T2EA model, the deployed continuous monitoring platform can collect kinds of attack related information to find and fix cyber attack. The useful information can be regard as the source of threat intelligence platform. By making full of threat intelligence information, the output knowledge can be used to track and target the attackers, and also can be seem as the input of comprehensive response platform to engage and assess the security systems and information infrastructure. Considering about this, we used a model to get local advantage in cyber security situation. The model is shown in Fig. 1.

In Find step of this model, we can get helpful information from suspicious alarm, vulnerability disclosure, NIDS (Network Intrusion Detection System), abnormal behavior detection, malware detection, threat intelligence platform and audit log during the seven phases of kill chains. In Fix step, security reinforce scheme refers to assets vulnerability management, NIDS, malware alarm, active report and abnormal behavior alarm, etc. In order to track and target the attackers, we can use flow analysis, log analysis, reverse analysis, trace back, honeypot and expert analysis, etc. In Engage step, responses and solutions include: black and white list, vulnerability mending, IPS (Intrusion Prevention System), anti-malware, DEP (Data Execution Prevention), process and authority protection, DNS redirect filtering, internal intrusion block, and forensic, etc. In final Assess step, assess measures need to be taken, including damage evaluation, threat intelligence sharing, emergency response drill, security education and training, management flow optimization and protection mechanism adjustment, etc.

	Find	Fix	Track	Target	Engage	Assess
Reconnaissance	Alarm				Black/White list	Damage evaluation
Weaponization	Vulnerability disclosure NIDS	Assets vulnerability management NIDS			Vulnerability mending IPS	Threat intelligence sharing
Delivery	Malware detection Active report	Malware alarm Active report	Flow analysis Log analysis	Log analysis	Anti-Malware Black/White list	Emergency response drill
Exploitation	Abnormal behavior detection	Abnormal behavior alarm	Log analysis	Log analysis	DEP Patch	Security education and training
Installation	Malware detection Abnormal behavior detection	Malware detection Abnormal behavior alarm	Log analysis Reverse analysis	Log analysis Reverse analysis	Anti-Malware Process & Authority protection	Management flow optimization
C2	External threat intelligence Abnormal behavior detection	External threat intelligence Abnormal behavior alarm	External threat intelligence Traceback	External threat intelligence Traceback	Black/White List DNS redirect filtering	Protection mechanism adjustment
Action on Objective	Abnormal behavior detection Audit log	Abnormal behavior alarm Audit log	Honeypot/Honeynet Expert analysis	Honeypot/Honeynet Expert analysis	Internal intrusion block Forensic	

Continuous Monitoring Platform ⇒ Threat Intelligence Platform ⇒ Comprehensive Response Platform

Fig. 1. Local advantage model based on threat intelligence

3.2 Framework of Cyber Attack Attribution

The framework of cyber attack attribution is used to describe the analysis procedure, platform construction and analysis content of cyber attack attribution. What's more, this framework can be regarded as the reference for schema design of actual deployment. The component of framework includes the start of analysis, the standard of threat intelligence, relevant data and systems of threat intelligence, evaluation of threat

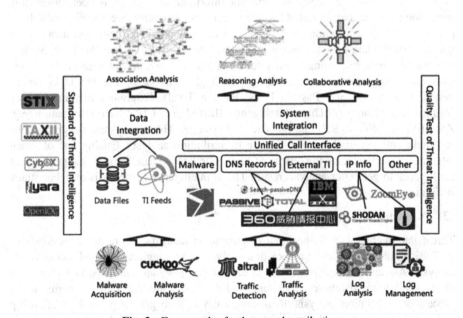

Fig. 2. Framework of cyber attack attribution

intelligence data and cyber attack attribution analysis. Figure 2 illustrates the framework of cyber attack attribution.

The framework is consists of three main parts: start of analysis, threat intelligence and attribution analysis. The internal components of every framework part and functionalities are discussed in the following:

(1) Start of analysis

According to the experience of emergency response and cyber-attack analysis, the original data mainly consist of three aspects: malware samples, network traffic and log records. In the course of the experiment, we can get malware from malware sample websites by web spider. Malware sandbox can be used to analyze the malicious activities of malwares, such as Cuckoo and ZeroWine, etc. Traffic detection and analysis are the main task of network traffic analysis. We can add evil IP address and domain name to black list to detect malicious behaviors. The association relation among the traffic data can be found by traffic analysis. Typical traffic detection and analysis software include Wireshark, Moloch, Malcon and Maltrail, etc. The tasks related to log include log management and analysis. The log records may contain users' access history, alarm information and operating records, etc. Powerful log management can provide effective in log analysis. Malware samples, network traffic and log records are the start of cyber attack attribution analysis.

(2) Threat intelligence

The task related to threat intelligence includes standard of threat intelligence, data integration, system integration and quality test of threat intelligence. Typical standards of threat intelligence include STIX (Structured Threat Information Expression), TAXII (Trusted Automated eXchange of Indicator Information), CybOX (Cyber Observable Expression), Yara and OpenIOC, etc. we can use and reference these standards in practical work of attribution analysis. Threat intelligence data integration means integrating various data files and threat intelligence feeds data to center database. System integration points that using unified call interface to integrate different kinds of systems, including malware detection system (e.g. VirusTotal), Passive DNS record system (e.g. Qihoo 360 Passive DNS, Passive Total), External threat intelligence platform (e.g. Qihoo 360 Threat Intelligence, IBM xForce.), IP related information (e.g. ZoomEye, Shodan, IVRE) and other related systems. Through system integration, we can make full use of threat intelligence in attribution analysis. Quality test of threat intelligence is to evaluate the quality of threat intelligence date from exchange of threat intelligence to get better analysis result. Threat intelligence is the basis of cyber attack attribution.

(3) Attribution analysis

Threat intelligence data is the input of attribution analysis. There are three kinds of attribution analysis methods: association analysis, reasoning analysis and collaborative analysis. Association analysis is to get as more as relevant and important data from threat intelligence database. Constraint and efficiency are the main concerns in the process of association analysis. Reasoning analysis is to get the possible relationship and attack chains from the associated data. The target of collaborative analysis is making full use of the performance of computer and the thinking of analysts in attribution analysis. Analysis is the main task in the process of cyber attack attribution.

This framework introduced the architecture of cyber attack attribution from the start of analysis to threat intelligence and analysis. From the framework, we can find out the process of cyber attack attribution and the related information and systems. At the same time, according to the framework, we can quickly build a testing environment to evaluate the effort of cyber attack attribution.

4 Case Study

In order to introduce the process and the framework of cyber attack attribution analysis, we used a practical case of cyber attack as follow. During the two meetings of China, there was a government website X had been attacked and some webpages had been distorted. Aiming at this situation, we started to investigate and analyze. The survey result shows that this organized attack was likely to be a targeted attack. The analysis processes are shown as follows:

(1) Website X had been attacked and its webpages had been distorted to objectionable content. We started the investigation and analysis.
(2) After detected the website and relevant severs, and analyzed the log files, we found that the website existed several vulnerabilities of Struct2 and SQL injection. We also found two suspicious executable files named "jpublish" and "syslogd" in server hosts. Their MD5 values are "d41d8cd98f00b204e9800998ecf8427e" and "4f1c0a24761deb8fd95e467add18a97f".
(3) At the same time, there were several severs exist more than two IP connections. Through network traffic capturing and analysis, we got two suspicious IP addresses: 122.10.41.105 and 122.10.13.99.
(4) By using the passive DNS systems integrated in threat intelligence platform, we reversely parsed the IP address and got the records. We can get the information about domain name, parsing type and the last parsing time. The parsing records are shown in Tables 1 and 2.
(5) According to registration related information of domain, we made an association analysis among these information data. Through the two IP addresses, we can find lot of possible associated information from threat intelligence data. Association graph is shown in Fig. 3.

Table 1. 122.10.13.99 parsing records

Domain	Type	Time
jbp567.com	A	2015-03-20 18:11:11
www.jbp234.com	A	2015-03-21 23:17:47
www.cp-cp.cc	A	2015-03-01 00:02:47
jbp234.com	A	2015-03-21 20:11:10
www.jbp345.com	A	2015-03-01 21:31:35
tt80001.com	A	2016-03-10 13:29:54

Table 2. 122.10.41.105 parsing records

Domain	Type	Time
caiyuanbc.com	A	2015-06-16 16:04:30
www.caiyuan1688.com	A	2015-06-03 16:13:41
www.zcedez.com	A	2015-09-21 14:05:06
www.bcpingji588.com	A	2015-09-30 07:41:43
www.osoomo.com	A	2015-09-08 10:13:59
ibaijiale.wang	A	2015-06-30 14:24:18
admin.skws4.dwmdph.com	A	2015-09-08 14:07:05
www.kpuduk.com	A	2015-09-08 00:19:06
www.zcogsz.com	A	2015-09-07 12:32:30
www.kqnhqb.com	A	2015-09-07 12:03:55
bak.888888k.com	A	2015-09-07 12:03:55
umikl.com	A	2010-03-55 12:57:48

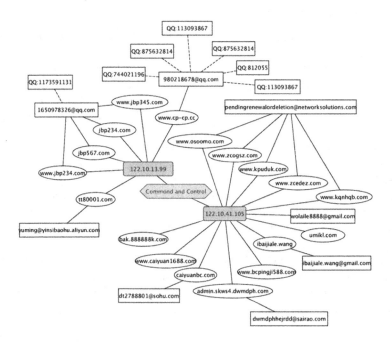

Fig. 3. Association graph

(6) By utilizing associated information in threat intelligence platform, we also built an association by STIX model. Through the STIX associated graph, we can clearly find out the attackers and attack process related information. The threat intelligence associated graph is shown in Fig. 4.

(7) By mapping the attack related information to the seven phases of kill chains and reasoning and supplying the miss clue and association, we can describe a

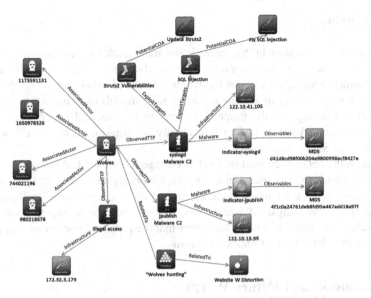

Fig. 4. Threat intelligence associated graph by STIX model

complete attack process. The parts with underline mean the reasoning and supplementing clues. The red dash arrow line means the association by reasoning. The red arrow line means mean the association by existing evidence. In this case, we found three suspicious threads in the whole attack process after analyzing and reasoning by the framework. The whole mapping and reasoning process is shown in Fig. 5.

Phase	Thread1	Thread2	Thread3
Reconnaissance	Scanning and detection		
Weaponization	Develop exploiting application Prepare exploit code		
Delivery	Webshell		IP:172.32.3.179
Exploitation	Struts2 vulnerabilities SQL injection		Privilege vulnerabilities
Installation	Jpublish	syslogd	
C2	122.10.13.99 [Heartbeat packets]	122.10.41.105 [Heartbeat packets]	
Action on Objectives	Website Distortion		Illegal Access

Fig. 5. Whole mapping and reasoning process.

5   Discussion

The main research content in this paper is the framework of cyber attack attribution. The theoretical basis of this framework is local advantage model. Through analyzing local advantage model, we can get the whole process of cyber attack and the related data in each stage. So we firstly researched existing models on cyber attack attribution analysis. Considering that the framework tends to the practical application, we subsequently researched industry solutions. Finally we determined to use threat intelligence in cyber attack attribution.

Because the detailed content of local advantage model and technology used in the framework are not the key points in this paper, we discussed little about them. In order to understand the process of cyber attack attribution based on threat intelligence, the paper combines the analysis of actual cases, so as to enhance the practical application of this value. The result of case study shows that the proposed framework can provide some help in cyber attack attribution analysis.

6   Conclusion and Future Works

According to the situation that current main security measures are accumulating security devices to protect relevant systems and networks, but the efforts is dissatisfied for advanced threats, we used an advantage model based on threat intelligence to deal with cyber attack. This model made full use of the constructed continuous monitoring platform, threat intelligence platform and comprehensive response platform to achieve the goals of early-warming, process detection and response and post attribution analysis through the seven steps of intrusion kill chains, and finally to reverse the security situation. We also came up with a framework of cyber attack attribution to describe the whole process of analysis. The framework introduced the related actions and resources in attribution analysis, including the start of analysis, the standard of threat intelligence, related data and systems of threat intelligence. Finally, we tested the model and framework by practical case. The case study indicated that the proposed framework and corresponding testing environment can provide some help in cyber attack attribution analysis. Framework of cyber attack attribution based on threat intelligence would be an effective architecture for cyber attack attribution.

In the future, our main energy focused on detailed technology and implements, especially automated analysis. Full-automated analysis would make full use of the advantage of threat intelligence data and platform, which could play an important role in cyber attack attribution analysis.

References

1. Trend Micro. Targetted Attacks (2016). http://www.trendmicro.com/vinfo/us/security/definition/targeted-attacks
2. Wheeler, D.A., Larsen, G.N.: Techniques for cyber attack attribution. No. IDA-P-3792. Institute for Defense Analyses, Alexandria, VA (2003)
3. Ryu, J., Na, J.: Security requirement for cyber attack traceback. In: Fourth International Conference on Networked Computing and Advanced Information Management, NCM 2008, vol. 2. IEEE (2008)
4. Hunker, J., Hutchinson, B., Margulies, J.: Role and challenges for sufficient cyber-attack attribution. In: Institute for Information Infrastructure Protection, pp. 5–10 (2008)
5. Tony Code. Attributions and Arrests: Lessons from Chinese Hacker (2015). https://www.fireeye.com/blog/executive-perspective/2015/12/attributions_andarr.html
6. Gartner. Definition: Threat Intelligence (2013). https://www.gartner.com/doc/2487216/definition-threat-intelligence
7. Gervais, P.: Nine Cyber Security Trends for 2016 (2015). http://www.prweb.com/releases/2015/12/prweb13125922.htm
8. Tirpak, J.A.: Find, fix, track, target, engage, assess. Air Force Mag. 83(7), 24–29 (2000)
9. U.S. Department of Defence. Joint Publication 3-60 Joint Targeting (2007). http://www.bits.de/NRANEU/others/jp-doctrine/jp3_60(07).pdf
10. Hutchins, E.M., Cloppert, M.J., Amin, R.M.: Intelligence-driven computer network defense informed by analysis of adversary campaigns and intrusion kill chains. In: Leading Issues in Information Warfare and Security Research, vol. 1, p. 80 (2011)
11. Caltagirone, S., Pendergast, A., Betz, C.: The diamond model of intrusion analysis. In: Center for Cyber Intelligence Analysis and Threat Research, Hanover, MD (2013)
12. Rid, T., Buchanan, B.: Attributing cyber attacks. J. Strateg. Stud. 38(1-2), 4–37 (2015)
13. Kaspersky. Kaspersky Lab Technology Leadership (2014). http://www.kaspersky.com/other/custom-html/b2b-ddos-prevention/pdf/kaspersky-technology-leadership.pdf
14. Kaspersky. Kaspersky Security Intelligence Services (2014). http://media.kaspersky.com/en/business-security/enterprise/Kaspersky_Security_Intelligence_Services_Threat_Intelligence_Services.pdf
15. FireEye. FireEye Threat Intelligence Engine (2015). https://www.fireeye.com/products/dynamic-threat-intelligence/threat-intelligence-engine.html
16. FireEye. FireEye Intelligence Center (2015). https://www.fireeye.com/content/dam/fireeye-www/global/en/products/pdfs/ds-fireeye-intelligence-center.pdf
17. Dell SecureWorks. Ever-Evolving Security Threat Landscape (2014). http://www.isaca.org/chapters3/Atlanta/AboutOurChapter/Documents/ISACAATL-062014-EverevolvingSecurityThreatLandscape.pdf
18. Dell SecureWorks. Counter Threat Platform (2016). https://www.secureworks.com/capabilities/counter-threat-platform
19. IBM Security. IBM X-Force Threat Intelligence (2016). http://www-03.ibm.com/security/xforce/
20. Qiang, L., et al.: A reasoning method of cyber-attack attribution based on threat intelligence. World Acad. Sci. Eng. Technol. Int. J. Comput. Electr. Autom. Control Inf. Eng. 10(5), 773–777 (2016)

UML Modeling of Cross-Layer Attack in Wireless Sensor Networks

Jian Wang[1]([⊠]), Abraham O. Fapojuwo[2], Chen Zhang[1],
and Huiting Tan[1]

[1] School of Electronic Science and Engineering,
National University of Defense Technology, Changsha, China
jwang@nudt.edu.cn
[2] Department of Electrical and Computer Engineering,
University of Calgary, Calgary, Canada
fapojuwo@ucalgary.ca

Abstract. The openness of wireless communication and the unattended nature of sensor node deployment make it easy for an adversary to launch various attacks on wireless sensor networks. Cross-layer attack aims to achieve better attack effects, conceal attack behavior more better, reduce the cost of attack by using information from multiple protocol layers, or initiate attack at multiple layers cooperatively. There are now different understandings about cross-layer attack. In this paper, the definition of cross-layer attack is proposed and several cases of attacks are presented. In order to better understand their behaviors, the cases of cross-layer attack are modeled by utilizing unified modeling language, which helps to build more secure wireless sensor networks.

Keywords: Cross-layer attack · Unified modeling language · Wireless sensor networks

1 Introduction

Wireless sensor networks (WSNs) are growing enormously and widely used in a broad range of fields, such as industry, agriculture, city control, medical treatment and environmental monitoring. As one of the key elements of the Internet of Things, WSNs help to obtain information for the Internet of Things. WSNs are composed of a large number of micro and low-power and low-priced sensor nodes deployed in sensing fields. By the method of wireless communication, these sensor nodes form a self-organized, self-adapted, and multi-hopped intelligent network system and transmit sensed information to the processing center through the base station. Different from other wireless communication networks, the resources of WSNs nodes, such as computation, storage, communication and energy, are limited and the sensor nodes are commonly deployed in unattended areas where the battery can neither be replaced nor recharged.

In view of the limitation of the resources of sensor nodes, the high-strength security mechanisms cannot be implemented in WSNs. Due to the openness of the deployment of nodes, the sensor nodes might be captured by the attacker and the sensitive information might be leaked or compromised. Thus, WSNs are facing more serious security

© ICST Institute for Computer Sciences, Social Informatics and Telecommunications Engineering 2017
N. Mitton et al. (Eds.): InterIoT 2016/SaSeIot 2016, LNICST 190, pp. 104–115, 2017.
DOI: 10.1007/978-3-319-52727-7_12

problems than the common traditional wireless networks, such as cellular networks. WSNs are susceptible to many different types of attacks at all layers of communication. An attacker can launch jamming [1] and tampering attacks [2, 3] at the physical layer. Attacks at the data link layer include collision [4], denial of sleep [5], Guaranteed Time Slot (GTS) attack [6], back-off manipulation [6] etc. The network layer of WSNs is vulnerable to different attacks, such as spoofed routing information [8], selective packet forwarding [8], sinkhole [8], wormhole [9], blackhole [10], sybil [11], hello flood [8], etc. Flooding attack and de-synchronization attack [1] are the attacks launched from the transport layer.

Besides the attacks directed to a single protocol layer, there are cross-layer attacks which relate to multiple layers in WSNs. Cross-layer attack can launch from one layer but aimed to another layer, use the information of one layer to produce an attack on another layer, or initiate at multiple layers cooperatively. The objectives of cross-layer attack are to achieve better attack effects, conceal attack behavior more better, or reduce the cost of attack. There are many different understandings about cross-layer attack [12–20]. In order to develop secure mechanism for WSNs, it is important to have a better understanding of cross-layer attack.

In this paper, cross-layer attacks in WSNs are studied at great depth. The main contributions of this paper are twofold. First, we propose a new definition of cross-layer attack and present several cases in different scenarios. Second, to better describe the behaviors of cross-layer attacks, we use Unified Modeling Language (UML) as the modeling framework.

The rest of this paper is organized as follows. Section 2 summarizes the related works about cross-layer attacks and propose a new definition of cross-layer attack. Section 3 presents the cases of cross-layer attack and its model. Finally, Sect. 4 concludes the paper.

2 Cross-Layer Attack in WSNs

The objectives of an attacker are to disrupt the security attributes of WSNs, including confidentiality, integrity, availability and authentication. To achieve these objectives, an adversary can launch attacks from different protocol layers of WSNs. At the physical layer, the adversary can jam the physical channel by interfering with the radio frequencies that nodes use for communication. Due to the unattended and distributed nature of deployment, the adversary can extract the secret information from the captured node, tamper with its circuitry, modify the program codes, or even replace it with malicious sensor [2, 3]. Data link layer is primarily responsible for medium access control, error control and frame detection. Attacks at the data link layer aim to disrupt the availability of the network by purposefully creating collisions, obtain unfair priority in the contention of channel or dissipate the limited energy of nodes. Network layer is primarily responsible for packet delivery including routing through intermediate nodes. Attacks at this layer aim to disrupt the network routing, acquire or control the data flows. Attacks at the transport layer aim to affect the data transmission by disrupting the existing connection or exhausting the connection resources. As described above, an attacker can achieve different goals by launching attack from different protocol layers. Actually, the attacker may not just restrict his attack at one layer.

Some previous works have been done in the area of cross-layer attack in WSNs [12–20]. Radosavac et al. considered a kind of cross-layer attack which propagated from Medium Access Control (MAC) layer to routing layer, causing serious degradation of network performance [12]. In their scenario, an attacker utilizes legitimate communication patterns in MAC layer to isolate one or multiple nodes in the network and break existing paths in the routing layer. Thus, the attacker increases the probability of including himself in the new routes. Bian et al. described the Stasis Trap attack that is launched from the MAC layer but aims to degrade the end-to-end throughput of flows at the transport layer [13]. In this attack, the adversary periodically preempts the wireless channel by using a small Contention Window (CW) size in order to cause large variations in the Round Trip Time (RTT) of Transmission Control Protocol (TCP) flows. This in turn will cause the Retransmission Timeout (RTO) of the flows to expire and the congestion window size will be reduced to one and retransmit outstanding packets according to the congestion control mechanism. This chain of events will result in a significant drop in the throughput of flows. This kind of attack has very little effect on the MAC layer throughput and hence it is very hard to be detected at the MAC layer, but it can severely degrade end-to-end throughput. Nagireddygari and Thomas analyzed the MAC-TCP cross-layer attack in cognitive radio networks [14]. León et al. presented the Lion attack performed at the physical/link layer that affects the transport layer in cognitive radio networks [15]. This attack relies on specific jamming that forces frequent handoffs thus affecting the current TCP connections. Guang et al. presented shortcut attack and detour attack that originate at the MAC layer but aim to disrupt the performance of ad hoc routing mechanism [16]. Shao et al. discovered a cross-layer dropping attack against video steaming in Ad hoc networks [17]. An attacker can launch various packet dropping attacks at the network layer by exploiting the application layer knowledge without creating abnormal behavior. Panchenko et al. showed how application layer information can be used to speed up the attack on the network layer [18]. Wang et al. investigated the coordinated report false sensing attack (Physical layer) and small back-off window attack (MAC layer) in cognitive radio network and proposed a trust-based cross-layer defense framework [19]. Djahel et al. addressed a cross-layer attack targeting proactive routing protocols, which is launched at the routing level and reinforced at the MAC layer in order to amplify the resulting damage [20].

As described above, there are now different understandings about cross-layer attack. The attacks presented in [12–16], can be categorized as a kind of cross-layer attack which launches from one layer but aims to another layer. Obviously, there are associations between different layers of the network architecture and if an adversary launches an attack from one layer the performance of another layer is bound to be affected. However, in this kind of cross-layer attack, the effects on the layer at which the attack is initiated will be very limited, but it will have dramatic effects on the performance of another layer. Thus, it is not easy to detect the attack behavior at the layer, from which the attacker launches the attack. In [17, 18], the attacker can obtain information from one layer and then utilize it to initiate an attack at another layer. As a smart attacker, he can use the information acquired from different layers comprehensively and aim to achieve a better attack effects or conceal himself as far as possible.

In [19, 20], the adversary launched several attacks from different layers cooperatively in order to cause greater damage to the target. Wang et al. defined cross-layer attack as attack activities that are conducted coordinately in multiple network layers [19]. In our opinion, it is not necessary for cross-layer attack to enforce attack on multiple layers. An attack can also be categorized as cross-layer attack as long as it can create large effects on one layer through another layer. That is to say, for cross-layer attack, the adversary can initiate an attack at a single layer if he can achieve some special attack goals at multiple other layers. Different from the attacks against a single layer, by considering the situations of multiple layers cooperatively, cross-layer attack aims to reduce the probability of being detected, reduce the cost of attack or achieve the attack goals that may not be feasible by enforcing an attack on a single layer only. Based on the foregoing, we propose a new definition of cross-layer attack as

A cross-layer attack is a kind of attack that initiates at one protocol layer, or multiple protocol layers cooperatively, by considering vulnerabilities or information of multiple layers comprehensively, in order to achieve the attack goals that cannot be reached by only considering a single layer.

Actually, in the scenario of cross-layer attack that the attacker initiates attack at multiple layers, it is different from multi-layer attack. In multi-layer attack, the adversary should conduct attacks at multiple layers, however, it is not necessary that the attacks at different layers be cooperative, that is to say, they could be independent. For example, an attacker can execute Denial of Service (DOS) attack at the physical layer, MAC layer and network layer concurrently or alternately. If the attack on each layer is cooperative, it can be classified as cross-layer attack, otherwise it only belongs to multi-layer attack. In cross-layer attack, it is not necessary for the adversary to launch an attack from multiple layers. It can launch an attack from one layer but aimed to another layer and the attacks at different layers should be conducted cooperatively to achieve specific objectives. We will give some cases of cross-layer attack in WSNs in the following section.

3   Modeling of Cross-Layer Attacks

To defend cross-layer attack and design secure protocols in a WSN, it is important to understand the behaviors of cross-layer attack by building its behavioral model. The UML is a standard notation of real-world objects as a first step in developing an object-oriented design methodology. It is a language for specifying, visualizing, constructing, and documenting the artifacts and is used to evolve and derive the system. It presents a standard way to show interaction/behavior within the system. The UML provides a large set of diagrams, such as use case diagram, sequence diagram, activity diagram, state machine diagram, and deployment diagram to model the system behavior. We have selected the UML framework for modeling of cross-layer attacks because it provides security developers standardized methodologies for visualizing security attacks in WSNs. Some previous works have been done to describe the attacks at a single layer in WSNs using UML [21–23]. Uke et al. proposed behavioral modeling of physical and data link layer security attacks in WSNs using state machine diagram [21]. Pawar et al. presented behavioral modeling of WSNs MAC security attacks using sequence diagram [22]. Hong et al. provided standard models for security attacks by UML sequence diagrams to describe and analyze possible attacks in the network and transport layers [23]. However, to the best of our knowledge, little research has been done in modeling of cross-layer attack in WSNs. In this section, we will present several cases of cross-layer attack in different scenarios and use UML to model them. These UML models will help security developers better understand the behaviors of cross-layer attack and the interaction of the system in presence of these attacks and build more secure WSNs.

3.1 MAC-Network Cross-Layer Attack

Attack at the MAC layer primarily aims to acquire priority in the contention of channel, dissipate the energy of the nodes, or create DOS. An attacker can cause collisions with neighboring nodes by sending jamming packets. And he can also get unfair priority access to the channel by setting a small CW value in the back-off mechanism, or modifying the Network Allocation Vector (NAV) in Request To Send (RTS) or Clear To Send (CTS) frames to reserve a longer time duration. At the network layer, an attacker can make himself a part of the routing path by sending bogus Route Reply (RREP) messages, advertising good Link Quality Indicator (LQI), such as low latency, low packet loss rate and small hop count.

In the scenario as described in Fig. 1(a), legitimate node A is the routing node and the data from other legitimate nodes, such as nodes B and C, are passed through it. A malicious node M wants to be the routing node in place of node A. It initiates attacks at the MAC and network layer coordinately to make himself being the node on the routing path (see Fig. 1(b)) and then it can launch selective forwarding, blackhole attack, etc. Actually, there are many kinds of attacks against MAC layer and network layer, we only give one example.

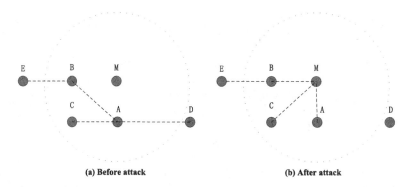

(a) Before attack   (b) After attack

Fig. 1. Scenario of MAC-Network cross-layer attack

Figure 2 shows the flow of events in case of this kind of cross-layer attack. The detailed procedures are as follows.

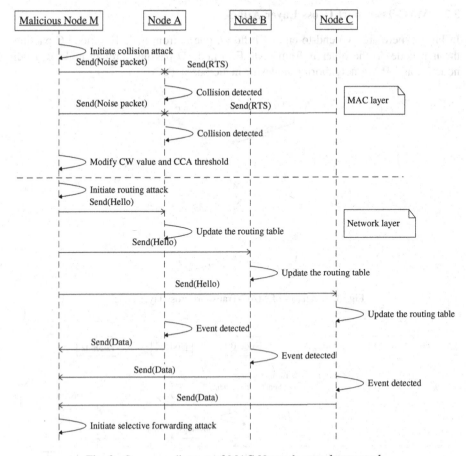

Fig. 2. Sequence diagram of MAC-Network cross-layer attack

(1) A malicious node M initiates collision attack on legitimate node A. When node B or C sends RTS to Node A, malicious node M generates a noise packet and sends it to node A at the same time. Both the packets will reach node A simultaneously and cause a collision. Thus, node B or C can hardly establish a channel with node A because the channel has been congested by malicious node M.

(2) Malicious node M modifies CW to a small value or increases its Clear Channel Assessment (CCA) threshold to a big value in order to acquire priority in the channel access.

(3) Malicious node M initiates routing attack by broadcasting bogus Hello message to the neighboring nodes. It advertises an attractive link quality for itself and the neighboring nodes take malicious node M as their new next hop routing node and update their routing Tables.

(4) The neighboring nodes detect the events and send their data to malicious node M. Thus, malicious node M can obtain the data of neighboring nodes and launch selective forwarding, blackhole attack, etc.

3.2   MAC-Transport Cross-Layer Attack

In Fig. 3, there are two end-to-end TCP flows, one is from node E to node C passing through node A, the other is from node F to node D passing through node B. Both nodes A and B are neighboring nodes of malicious node M.

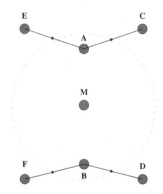

Fig. 3. Scenario of MAC-Transport cross-layer attack

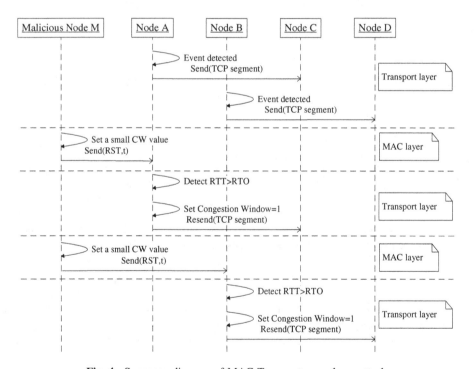

Fig. 4. Sequence diagram of MAC-Transport cross-layer attack

Malicious node M preempts the channel by manipulating the back-off mechanism at the MAC layer but its aim is to degrade the end-to-end throughput of flows at the transport layer [13]. Malicious node M manipulates the back-off values by using a small CW size and it can acquire the priority amongst all the contending nodes. Once the channel is preempted, malicious node M transmits data to node A or node B for a long enough period to cause noticeable delays in the TCP flows that are traversing through node A or B. According to the congestion control mechanism at the transport layer, if the RTT is delayed beyond the RTO, the congestion window size will be reduced to one and the outstanding packets will be retransmitted. Thus, the end-to-end throughput of the flows will be degraded seriously. Malicious node M preempts the channel periodically and switches transmission destination between node A and node B in a round-robin manner. It is very hard to detect the attack behavior at the MAC layer because it has very little effect on MAC layer throughput. The detailed procedures are as described in Fig. 4.

(1) Nodes A and B forward TCP segment to nodes C and D, respectively.
(2) Malicious node M sets a small CW size to acquire the priority in the contention of channel. It sends RTS frame to node A and the duration of occupying channel is *t* which is longer than the RTO.
(3) Node A detects that RTT is delayed beyond RTO and TCP sender will assume packet loss in this case. According to the congestion control mechanism, the congestion window value will be set to one and node A will retransmit the outstanding TCP segments.
(4) Malicious node M then switches the transmission destination to node B and performs the same operations on node B as it did to node A.
(5) Malicious node M periodically repeats the above steps (2)–(4).

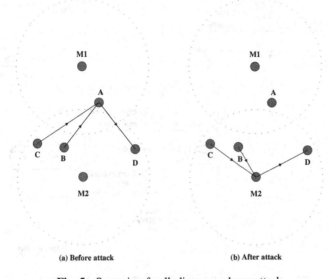

(a) Before attack   (b) After attack

Fig. 5. Scenario of colluding cross-layer attack

3.3 Colluding Cross-Layer Attack

Figure 5 describes a scenario that two malicious nodes M1 and M2 collude to launch an attack. In this scenario, nodes B, C and D are neighboring nodes of node A. In Fig. 5 (a), node A is the next hop routing node of nodes B and C and it forwards the data of nodes B and C to node D. Node A is in the range of M1 and nodes B and C are in the range of M2. In order to disrupt the routing, malicious node M1 initiates collision attack on node A at the MAC layer and then malicious node M2 launches routing attack on nodes B and C at the network layer. After the attack, M2 becomes the next hop routing node of nodes B and C (see in Fig. 5(b)). Hence, M1 can initiate selective forwarding attack at the network layer.

The detailed procedures are as follows, illustrated in Fig. 6.

(1) Malicious node M1 intercepts the routing information sent by node A and acquires the information that node A is an important routing node.
(2) In order to disrupt the network routing, M1 performs collision attack on node A at the MAC layer. When other nodes send data to node A, M1 sends jamming packet

Fig. 6. Sequence diagram of colluding cross-layer attack

at the same time and then causes collisions. If the data transmission are always failed, nodes B and C may select another node as their next hop routing node.

(3) Malicious node M2 advertises a high quality route to node D to attract the traffic by sending bogus routing information. Then nodes B and C update their routing table. M2 becomes the next hop routing node of nodes B and C.

(4) Nodes B and C detect the event and send their data to M2, which then selectively forwards their packets to node D.

4 Conclusion

To conceal attack behavior more better, in cross-layer attack, it usually has little effects on the parameters of one protocol layer. Thus, for intrusion detection system, it can hardly distinguish normal behavior from abnormal behavior at one protocol layer because the deviation of protocol parameter is very small under cross-layer attack. And even if the intrusion detection system observes the anomaly, it is not easy to decide at which layer that the attack initiated and hence hard to make a response. For example, the modification of CW value will not bring huge effects to the contention of channel at the MAC layer and small changes in routing information will not draw more attention by the monitoring node. A smart attacker then utilizes MAC-Network cross-layer attack to achieve better attack effects on WSNs and decreases the probability of being detected at a single protocol layer as far as possible.

To detect cross-layer attack, it is necessary to use cross-layer based detection approach. Detection system monitors the critical parameters of multiple layers, such as Received Signal Strength Indication, Energy Reduction Rate at the physical layer, Back-off Time, Packet Collision Rate at the data link layer, Link Quality Indicator, Hop Count at the network layer, Number of Connections, RTT at the transport layer, Type of Data at the application layer. It draws a conclusion whether there is an attack behavior by analyzing the deviation of the parameters of different layers cooperatively. That is to say, detection system should not only extract features from multiple layers but also consider the correlation between attacks in different layers.

Wireless sensor networks are vulnerable to many types of attacks at different protocol layers due to the openness of the wireless channel and deployment of sensor nodes in an unattended area. Different from the attacks just aiming at a single layer, in cross-layer attack, an attacker can utilize the information from different layers separately or initiate attack at different layers cooperatively, and then achieve the attack goal that cannot be reached by only considering a single layer. Different explanations about cross-layer attack in WSNs currently exist. In this paper, we tried to study the objectives and behaviors of cross-layer attack and presented the definition of cross-layer attack. In order to better understand the behavior of cross-layer attack, we put forward several cases of cross-layer attacks and utilized sequence diagram to model them. These sequence diagrams show the attack's behaviors and the interactions between different objects in a network, which will be beneficial for developing secure solutions for WSNs. It is interesting to use other diagrams, such as activity diagram, state machine diagram, to model cross-layer attack in the future. The objective of investigating attack's behaviors is to detect them. In future works, we will focus on how to design the structure of detection system in WSNs, how to deploy it and how to design effective cross-layer attack detection algorithms.

References

1. Wood, A.D., Stankvic, J.A.: Denial of service in sensor networks. IEEE Comput. **35**(10), 54–62 (2002)
2. Wang, X., Gu, W., Schosek, K., Chellappan, S., Xuan, D.: Sensor network configuration under physical attacks. Technical Report:OSU-CISRC-7/04-TR45, Department of Computer Science and Engineering, Ohio State University (2004)
3. Katsaiti, M., Rigas, A., Tzemos, I., Sklavos, N.: Real-world attacks toward circuits and systems design, targeting safety invasion. In: Proceedings of the 4th International Conference on Modern Circuits and System Technologies (MOCAST) (2015)
4. Xu, W., Ma, K., Trappe, W., Zhang, Y.: Jamming sensor networks: attack and defense strategies. IEEE Netw. **20**(3), 41–47 (2006)
5. Raymond, D.R., Marchany, R.C., Brownfield, M.I., Midkiff, S.F.: Effects of Denial-of sleep attacks on wireless sensor network MAC protocols. IEEE Trans. Veh. Technol. **58**(1), 367–380 (2009)
6. Sokullu, R., Dagdeviren, O., Korkmaz, I.: On the IEEE 802.15.4 MAC layer attacks: GTS attack. In: Proceedings of the Second International Conference on Sensor Technologies and Applications (SENSORCOMM), pp. 673–678 (2008)
7. Radosavac, S., Crdenas, A.A., Baras, J.S., Moustakides, G.V.: Detecting IEEE 802.11 MAC layer misbehavior in ad hoc networks: robust strategies against individual and colluding attackers. J. Comput. Secur. **15**(1), 103–128 (2007). Special Issue on Security of Ad Hoc and SensorNetworks
8. Karlof, C., Wagner, D.: Secure routing in wireless sensor networks: attacks and countermeasures. Ad Hoc Netw. J. **1**(2–3), 293–315 (2003)
9. Hu, Y.C., Perrig, A., Johnson, D.B.: Packet Leashes: a defense against wormhole attacks in wireless networks. In: Proceedings of the Twenty-Second Annual Joint Conference of the IEEE Computer and Communication Societies (INFOCOM), vol. 3, pp. 1976–1986 (2003)
10. Al-Shurman, M., Yoo, S.M., Park, S.: Black hole attack in mobile Ad hoc networks. In: Proceedings of the 42nd Annual ACM Southeast Regional Conference (ACM-SE'42) (2004)
11. Newsome, J., Shi, E., Song, D., Perrig, A.: The Sybil attack in sensor networks: analysis & defenses. In: Proceedings of the Third International Symposium on Information Processing in Sensor Networks ACM (IPSN), pp. 259–268 (2004)
12. Radosavac, S., Benammar, N., Baras, J.S.: Cross-layer attacks in wireless ad hoc networks. In: Proceedings of the 38th Annual Conference on Information Science and Systems (CISS). Princeton University (2004)
13. Bian, K., Park, J.M., Chen, R.: Stasis Trap: cross-layer stealthy attack in wireless Ad hoc networks. In: Proceedings of the IEEE Global Telecommunications Conference (GLOBE-COM) (2006)
14. Nagireddygari, D., Thomas, J.: MAC-TCP cross-layer attack and its defense in cognitive radio networks. In Proceedings of the 10th ACM International Symposium on QOS and Security for Wireless and Mobile Networks (Q2SWinet) (2014)

15. León, O., Hernández-Serrano, J., Soriano, M.: A new cross-layer attack to TCP in cognitive radio network. In: Proceedings of the Second International Workshop on Cross layer Design (IWCLD) (2009)
16. Guang, L., Assi, C., Benslimane, A.: Interlayer attacks in mobile Ad hoc networks. In: Cao, J., Stojmenovic, I., Jia, X., Das, Sajal, K. (eds.) MSN 2006. LNCS, vol. 4325, pp. 436–448. Springer, Heidelberg (2006). doi:10.1007/11943952_37
17. Shao, M., Zhu, S., Cao, G., Porta, T.L., Mohapatra, P.: A cross-layer dropping attack in video streaming over Ad hoc networks. In: Proceedings of the 4th International Conference on Security and Privacy in Communication Networks (SECURECOMM) (2008)
18. Panchenko, A., Pimenidis, L.: Cross-layer attack on anonymizing networks. In: Proceedings of the 15th International Conference on Telecommunication (ICT) (2008)
19. Wang, W., Sun, Y., Li, H., Han, Z.: Cross-layer attack and defense in cognitive radio networks. In: Proceedings of IEEE Global Telecommunication Conference (GLOBECOM) (2010)
20. Djahel, S., Abdesselam, F.N., Khokhar, A.: A cross layer framework to mitigate a joint MAC and routing attack in multihop wireless network. In: Proceedings of the 5th IEEE International Workshop on Performance and Management of Wireless and Mobile Networks (P2MNET) (2009)
21. Uke, S.N., Mahajan, A.R., Thool, R.C.: UML modeling of physical and data link layer security attacks in WSN. Int. J. Comput. Appl. 70(11), 25–28 (2013)
22. Pawar, P.M., Nielsen, R.H., Prasad, N.R., Ohmori, S., Prasad, R.: Behavioral modeling of WSN MAC layer security attacks: a sequential UML approach. J. Cyber Secur. Mob. 1(1), 65–82 (2012)
23. Hong, S., Lim, S.: Analysis of attack models via unified modeling language in wireless sensor networks: a survey study. In: Proceedings of IEEE International Conference on Wireless Communications, Networking and Information Security (WCINS) (2010)

Adoption of Miniaturized Safety-Related Systems for Industrial Internet-of-Things Applications

Ali Hayek[✉], Samer Telawi, Christian Bieler, and Josef Börcsök

Chair for Computer Architecture and System Programming,
University of Kassel, Wilhelmshoeher Allee 71, 34121 Kassel, Germany
ali.hayek@uni-kassel.de

Abstract. Nowadays the internet is considered as given in almost any consumer electronic application. Internet connections are now extended to physical objects and are able to connect the living environment with computers, laptops, tablets and smartphones. We are dealing here with the Internet of Things. However, it is only the beginning of the Internet of Things revolution and today the development process has entered a new stage, where Internet of Things includes more and more industrial devices. Of course, using Internet of Things in such application fields faces the challenge of balancing the flexibility of internet communication and the robustness of industrial applications. In this paper, a concept of the adoption of a miniaturized safety-related solution on a single chip for industrial Internet of Things applications is introduced. An example application is presented to prove the feasibility of the introduced concept.

Keywords: Internet of Things · Safety systems · Systems-on-Chip · Wireless network

1 Introduction

Intelligent computer systems, peripheral devices of any type such as mobile devices, sensors, machines and vehicles are networked with each other and with the external environment by means of the Internet of Things (IoT). The analysis of the IoT data offers many opportunities for companies to exploit, such as taking faster decisions, better optimization and refinement of their business processes, revealing new applications and even the development of new business models. IoT thus offers enormous potentials for almost any technical field as energy technology, industrial automation and factory, medical technology, automotive industry as well as production and logistics.

Against this background, IoT applications can mainly be divided into two categories. On one hand, there is IoT applied to consumer electronics (CIoT), and on another hand, there is the industrial IoT (IIoT). CIoT devices represent consumer-oriented applications such as big and small household appliances that are usually communicating with small data volumes and low data rates but they are not used in safety or mission critical applications. Whereas, IIoT devices represent industry-oriented applications, e.g. machines and robots in an industrial environment in which

© ICST Institute for Computer Sciences, Social Informatics and Telecommunications Engineering 2017
N. Mitton et al. (Eds.): InterIoT 2016/SaSeIot 2016, LNICST 190, pp. 116–126, 2017.
DOI: 10.1007/978-3-319-52727-7_13

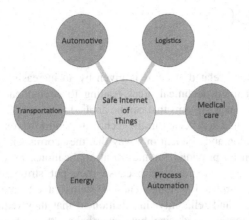

Fig. 1. Application fields of the Safe Internet of Things

they communicate with higher data volumes and rates. Furthermore, IIoT applications have normally to be classified as safety and reliability critical. In this context Fig. 1 provides an overview of the most important fields that can involve IIoT devices in safety-related applications (Safe Internet of Things).

According to the most common definition, the IoT is a network of physical things, which are different embedded electronic parts such as sensors, microcontrollers and communication interfaces to collect and exchange data [1]. Moreover, adopting these things is getting more widely in the industrial environments to fulfill more critical tasks that are related to monitoring performance and safety of workers, machines or any other important factor in the industrial environment. Furthermore, enormous efforts have been conducted to safely monitor and manage the industrial environments such as the research work conducted by Alcaraz and Lopez [2, 3], in which they introduce a system that utilizes many technologies, and the wireless sensors are a main part of these solutions. In order to provide a safe sensory data, which is the main effort of this research work, the wireless sensory system must comply one of the safety-related architectures adopted in the safety-related digital systems [4, 5].

Consequently, such a linkage between safety-related systems and IoT devices is not well-engineered yet; and this requires implementing a safety-related architecture for the whole path of the captured data, starting from the sensors to the end point to which the data is transmitted. Some challenges, as system size, costs and ensuring the high level of safety and resilience, have still to be mastered. In this work, consistently with our own research work about the realization of on-chip safety systems a concept is presented, which focuses on the realization of applying miniaturized IIoT systems to safety-related applications. The objective in this context is to establish miniaturized as well as robust, flexible and efficient systems for the use in IIoT devices.

The paper is organized as the following. Section 2 provides an overview of the state of the art of safety-related systems and on-chip safety systems. Section 3 serves to introduce the concept of adapting an on-chip safety system to IIoT applications. Initial results are presented through the use of an example application in Sect. 4. Finally, a summary and an outlook serve to round off this paper.

2 Safety Systems

2.1 Introduction

The relevance of safety-related systems is given by an increasingly growing level of safety awareness in many technical areas leading to strengthened requirements for standardized safety-related systems that can be applied to various fields of applications. Moreover, this relevance is reflected in the technical trend towards safety systems that are increasingly flexible and efficient in a way that they correspond to the current state of the art which can be provided for industrial applications. Furthermore, economic considerations do play a major role because they put stringent demands on the development of safety-related systems. These systems have to meet the key requirements, such as safety and reliability, in addition to that they require several further characteristics like miniaturized size but nevertheless they also require maximum performance and lower costs as well as the highest level of flexibility and portability at the same time. The latter aspect is particularly important due to the connection with applications in the field of Industry 4.0 and the IIoT.

In recent years, based on the previously mentioned background, more new technological platforms have been increasingly used to realize safety-related systems. Conventional hard-wired controllers have been replaced by electronic and programmable controllers. The current trend in this field is characterized by two important aspects: One aspect is to make use of the technical progress that results from the development within the field of semiconductor technology and the other aspect is to allow that given state of the development an appropriate corresponding state of standardization. In fact, the safety-related electronic systems have undergone a significant development over the last few years. A decisive milestone in this area has been achieved, especially with the release of the second edition of the standard IEC 61508 [6] and the associated introduction of safety-related systems involving on-chip redundancy. Safety-related systems with two redundant channels can now be developed on one single chip and certified in accordance with standard IEC 61508.

The following subsections provide a rough overview of the standard IEC 61508 and its development. Subsequently, a brief outline is given about on-chip safety systems that are proposed to be used for the realization of the introduced concept.

2.2 Safety Standard IEC 61508

In this section a brief insight into the safety standard IEC 61508 is introduced. The standard IEC 61508 is limited to electrical/electronic/programmable electronic safety-related systems – short form E/E/PE. It is divided into seven parts and deals with the general requirements for the development process of safety-related systems at hardware and software levels. Furthermore, the standard serves to define key terms like functional safety or safety integrity level (SIL), which serves for a classification of safety-related systems. The safety-related systems are classified into four levels SIL 1 to SIL 4. It applies here that the higher the SIL, the safer the system under consideration. In addition, the standard provides different parameters to be used for a quantitative evaluation of various safety architectures. Finally, examples and operating instructions for the determination of the safety integrity level as well as for the way to use the different architectures, procedures and measures are provided by the standard.

For the on-chip safety systems that are proposed in this research work, the second edition of that standard of the year 2010 is of great significance. Among other things, the on-chip redundancy, which provides the possibility to develop safety-related systems on a single silicon substrate for SIL 3 applications, was introduced in this edition.

2.3 On-Chip Safety Systems

Besides the key requirements like networkability, reliability and robustness, further requirements do also play a significant role for IIoT applications, especially in the case of the embedded applications, where the compact system size and reduced power loss at an optimized performance, represent the key factors for technical and economic considerations. The conventional technique, which was used for safety-related systems, has considered these factors solely in a very limited way. Therefore, only when the on-chip redundancy in the IEC 61508 was introduced; a safety-related basis has been established for that. At that point the standard provides a roadmap for the development of safety-related systems on a single silicon chip. In fact, since the introduction of that standard, the trend was towards an integration of complete control systems on the smallest silicon areas. Several semiconductor manufacturers and safety experts like Texas Instruments, Freescale or Yogitech have also brought dozens of such solutions to the market ever since, and an overview on the previously existing safety chips is provided in [7]. For the purpose of realizing systems with on-chip redundancy measures, methods and modelling techniques, that should serve to guarantee the technical safety, have to be provided at all levels of development. These comprehensive measures have to be taken on the modelling level as well as on the chip design level. In [8] a summarized overview of these required measures is introduced. In the following subsection, an example is given, which is based on an own previously published architecture, and it serves to illustrate how a safety controller works on a chip. The introduced architecture serves as a basis for the research concept that is presented in this paper.

2.4 On-Chip Safety Architecture

The presented architecture is based primarily on 1oo2D architecture (one out of two with Diagnosis). The 1oo2D architecture according to standard IEC 61508 consists of a simple redundant architecture including two channels and additional diagnosis. In a 1oo2D architecture a dangerous failure can only occur if both channels do create a dangerous failure. The system can fail, only if a dangerous error has occurred in both channels. As a mean of increasing the flexibility of this architecture, it is extended by a communication processor, which serves as a black communication channel. This channel is not interacting with the safe system (interference free communication channel). Figure 2 illustrates a block diagram of this architecture which is represented in the green box on both sides of the figure. The design, which is in accordance with

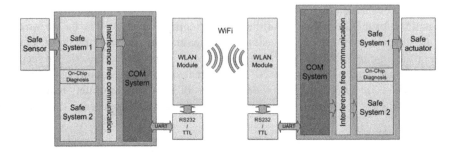

Fig. 2. Block diagram of the IIoT-Enabled on-chip safety system

IEC 61508 second edition representing a safety solution with on-chip redundancy has already been implemented and published in [9].

3   IIoT-Enabled Safety System

3.1   System Architecture

As already been outlined in the previous sections, the basic idea of the current concept is to use an on-chip safety system for safety-related IIoT applications. In this context, the focus is led on using a flexible and miniaturized safety system, which is appropriate for applications that place stringent demands on particularly the system size and costs.

Figure 2 above serves to illustrate a block diagram dealing with a possible implementation of the research project. This implementation adopts the Safe-Device-to-Safe-Device communication model and the on-chip safety system represents the heart of it. The most important features of this on-chip system are the ability to process safe inputs like input sensory data and to allow safe outputs such as actuator data. In this case, the communication of IoT applications is conducted via wireless LAN. At this point, the communication could also be realized via Ethernet or any other wireless communication like RFM radio modules; a concept that utilizes RFM modules will be presented later on. In addition, any communication model of IoT could be adopted such as Device-to-Cloud model or Device-to-Gateway model with respect to safety-related aspects [10]. The following sections deal in more detail with the single components of the introduced system.

3.2   Target on-Chip Safety System

The target on-chip safety system is a miniaturized SIL 3 compliant architecture which integrates all features of a PLC on a single chip. This reduces the number of required components for safety applications and improves system dependability. A more detailed description of this architecture can be found in [9]. Figure 2 gives a general overview about the system architecture of the safety PLC, which consists of two subsystems: a redundant system (1oo2D safe system) and a single-core system intended for communication (COM system). Both subsystems are connected via interference-free channel. In addition, both processor systems may trigger an interrupt in the other sub-system. Both subsystems contain processor cores with their own data and program memories, digital inputs and outputs, as well as diverse communication interfaces. The COM system acts as black channel for safe communication between the safe system and the devices of safety-related applications, through utilizing its communication interfaces such as serial interfaces and Ethernet.

3.3 WLAN Module

The ESP8266 WLAN module [11] is used in this research work, and it has been successfully marketed in different versions by the company Espressif for some time. The modules typically consist of the system-on-chip SoC ESP8266EX, an external Flash RAM and an antenna or an antenna interface. The modules mainly differ according to the number of interfaces that are available to the exterior. The smallest configuration ESP8266-01 including 8 pins is used for the present research work. It is also important to note at that point that WLAN modules of other manufacturers or other wireless communication interfaces can also be used.

The module ESP8266-01 represents the smallest module of the ESP8266 WIFI family. The structure is roughly presented in Fig. 3 which shows its components that are consisting of a 32 bit RISC SoC (Tensilica L106) with integrated analog/RF transceiver, Flash RAM memory and an antenna that is integrated on the board. The module is produced by Espressif in China. Having a size of 5×5 mm for the SoC and 1.5×2.5 cm for the module it involves rather low manufacturing costs. Due to its low power consumption of a maximum of 215 mA and less than 1 mA in stand-by mode, furthermore, its small size and high performance, the module is not only suited for being used as a WLAN module but also for being used as complete solution for IoT applications. The firmware can be freely programmed and only 20% of the possible computational power is consumed during the WIFI operation. Consequently 80% of the performance is theoretically available for user applications. Version ESP8266-01 provides to the user, alongside with the SoC, an external Flash and an antenna, 8 pins,

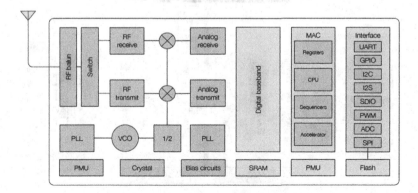

Fig. 3. Block diagram of WLAN module ESP8266EX [11]

too. The pins are required for the power supply, reset, chip-enable, firmware programming and the communication via UART. The firmware is externally loaded via SPI from Flash and it can be reprogrammed by the use of the UART interface.

4 Communication Network and IoT Application

The main purpose of the example application in this paper is to present a prototype platform for processing safe sensor data using a miniaturized safety system and transferring this data via wireless communication to other IoT devices. As already mentioned in the previous section, the safety system consists of a redundant processor system with integrated diagnostic units, and a communication system that serves as a black interference-free communication channel. The data that have been read out is processed and delivered to the RS232/TTL converter through a serial UART interface of the communication system. The converter regulates the voltage so that it will go down to 3.3 V and it forwards the data to the used WLAN module. As soon as one complete line has been transmitted, the WLAN module is going to respond with an echo and a reply. The communication system will then be in a position to verify whether the data were transferred correctly.

4.1 Example Test Design

Besides the module ESP8266-01, power supply, an RS232/TTL (15 V/3.3 V) converter and the system that communicates with the chip, are necessary for the experimental setup. Moreover, a button is used for the reset. An AMS1117 3.3 with 3.3 V is used for the power supply of the WLAN module and an AMS1117 5.0 with 5 V of Advanced Monolithic is used for the RS232-TTL converter. The RS232/TTL converter is an MAX2323 module from the company Maxim and has to be operated with 5 V. It should be noted that all modules share a common ground so that disturbances can be

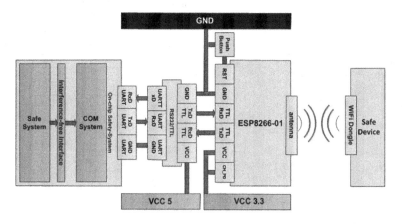

Fig. 4. Block diagram of a simple test design

prevented. The RxD/TxD signals are connected crosswise at the modules. The Baud rate is set to 115200Bd at all systems.

As soon as the system is switched on, the ESP8266-01 can be configured. The standard firmware runs with the AT-Instruction-Set. A connection between the safety system and the module has to be established via the UART interface. By entering "AT\r\n" it is tested whether the module is ready. If the answer "AT\r\nOK\r\n" is received, the system will be ready. Further information on additional commands can be found in the ESP8266 AT Instruction Set Version 1.5.4 on the website of Espressif [12]. The WLAN module can be configured as station, access point or as both at the same time. Figure 4 illustrates the block diagram of a simple test design.

4.2 Results and Evaluation

After having introduced the test setup in the previous section, the current section will be dealing with a brief introduction of the first results that have been obtained. An initial feasibility study has been carried out along with the introduced demo design. In this context, a validated Field Programmable Gate Array (FPGA) platform as realized served as prototype platform for the used on-chip safety system. A connection of the WLAN interface to the serial interface of the communication system has been realized and wireless communications with a host computer have been established successfully. Figure 5 shows a photo of the realized prototype.

Thus the first step in realizing the proposed concept was taken. Two crucial aspects have to be emphasized regarding future work. On one hand, there is the miniaturization of the system where the on -chip safety system is integrated together with the WLAN module on the smallest hardware structure, and on other hand there is the important aspect of dealing with the ability to guarantee a safe wireless communication, because without this aspect a complete system safety could not be achieved.

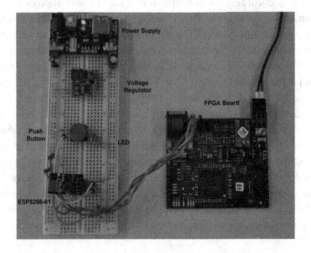

Fig. 5. Hardware prototyping platform with WLAN module and FPGA board

Miniaturization: A first hardware design has been implemented for the miniaturization of the test setup. Figure 6 shows the layout of the target hardware created in Cadence Allegro. The target hardware mainly consists of the on-chip safety system and the connection to the WLAN module. Further important units, among others, are the power supply and its monitoring as well as the circuit of an external Watchdog. Due to the size of 7 cm x 4 cm the realized design serves to provide the optimal platform for wireless, safe networks for IIoT applications. A long-term objective of our research work is to integrate the complete system on a single chip to achieve the first IIoT safety chip solution.

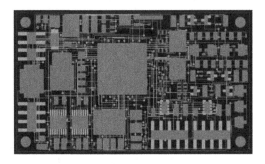

Fig. 6. Layout of an IIoT network

Wireless Safe Communication: For the purpose of ensuring a safe wireless communication, a significant addition to the introduced architecture is required. At first glance it seems as if there are two suitable options to provide conceivable solutions. Firstly, the wireless communication can be realized directly via the safety system, and secondly, it can be carried out in a redundant way via the communication processor. The first variant would imply two WLAN modules or two RF radio modules having two different frequencies, being connected to two serial interfaces or two SPI interfaces of the safety system accordingly. A conceptual diagram of this approach with both suggested communication modules is shown in Fig. 7. The advantage of this variant is that it results in two redundant communication channels that are processed by an equally redundant processor system. The technical challenges to be faced at that point would be the handling of the synchronization and the loss of performance at the safety system.

The second variant would imply two WLAN modules or two RF radio modules being connected to two different serial interfaces of the communication processor accordingly, exactly as shown in Fig. 7 above, but the communication modules will be connected to the communication system rather than to safe System. An appropriate comparison is also carried out there. The advantage of this variant is that the communication is still established via the communication processor and thus the performance of the safety system remains unaffected. However, a disadvantage is represented by the singularity of the communication processor. Diversity of the wireless interfaces e.g. using 2.4 GHz and 5 GHz and multiple comparisons depending on the targeted safety level represents appropriate measures to be adopted to solve this.

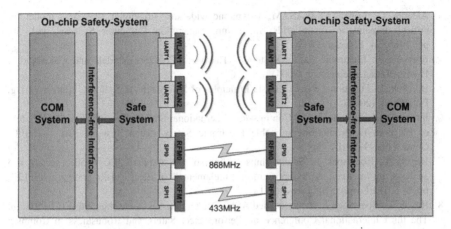

Fig. 7. Example layout of a safe IIoT network

In each case, a feasibly study for those proposed solutions and for other possible solutions will represent the main focus of further research on this topic, in addition to developing a suitable safe communication protocol to each suggested approach.

5 Conclusion

The background of IIoT and Industry 4.0 implies that better networking of industrial devices as well as increasing miniaturization and lower costs of hardware have to be achieved. In this context, the introduced concept presented in this work delivers a contribution to the realization of a miniaturized safety-related platform for the implementation in industrial IoT applications. The solution, which is presented in this paper, comprises the following steps: (1) Introducing an on-chip safety system, (2) Integrating wireless communication, (3) Designing a model for a communication network for safe IoT implementations and using example hardware. The presented solution represents a compact and flexible solution consisting of a miniaturized on-chip safety system and wireless communication for the use in safe industrial IoT applications. The feasibility of the presented example served to demonstrate the enormous potential of the IoT devices for the implementation in safety-related industrial applications. Furthermore, this paper deals with open suggestions for enhancements guaranteeing a safe communication, which are not yet fully developed. They are going to be elaborated and published within the scope of future research activities.

References

1. McEwen, A., Cassimally, H.: Designing the Internet of Things. Wiley, Chichester (2014)
2. Alcaraz, C., Lopez, J.: Diagnosis mechanism for accurate monitoring in critical infrastructure. Comput. Stand. Interfaces **36**(3), 501–512 (2014). Elsevier

3. Alcaraz, C., Lopez, J.: WASAM: a dynamic wide-area situational awareness model for critical domains in smart grids. In: Future Generation Computer Systems, vol. 30, pp. 146–154. Elsevier (2014)

4. Börcsök, J.: Electronic Safety Systems - Hardware Concepts Models and Calculations. Hüthig-Verlag, Heidelberg (2004)

5. Börcsök, J.: Functional Safety - Basic Principles of Safety-related Systems. Hüthig-Verlag, Heidelberg (2007)

6. International Electrotechnical Commission: International Standard: 61508 Functional Safety of Electrical/Electronic/Programmable Electronic Safety-related Systems Part 1–7. IEC, Geneva (1999–2010)

7. Hayek A., Boercsoek J.: Safety chips in light of the standard IEC 61508: survey and analysis. In: International Symposium on Fundamentals of Electrical Engineering (ISFEE), pp. 1–6. IEEE press, Bucharest (2014)

8. Hayek A., Boercsoek J.: Safety-related ASIC-Design in terms of the standard IEC 61508. In: The third International Conference on Performance, Safety and Robustness in Complex Systems and Applications (PESARO), pp. 16–21. IARIA press, Venice (2013)

9. Hayek A., Machmur B., Schreiber M., Boercsoek J.: Safety-related system-on-chip architecture for embedded computing applications. In: European Safety and Reliability Association Annual Conference (ESREL). ESRA press, Amsterdam (2013)

10. The Internet of Things: An Overview, Understanding the Issues and Challenges of a more Connected World (2015). http://www.internetsociety.org

11. Espressif Systems: Espressif Smart Connectivity Platform ESP8266. Espressif Systems Inc. (2013)

12. ESP8266 AT Instructions Set (2013). https://espressif.com/en/content/esp8266-instruction-set

Identifying DOS and DDOS Attack Origin: IP Traceback Methods Comparison and Evaluation for IoT

Brian Cusack[1(✉)], Zhuang Tian[1], and Ar Kar Kyaw[1,2]

[1] Digital Forensic Research Laboratory, School of Engineering Computer and Mathematical Science, Auckland University of Technology, 55 Wellesley Street East, Auckland, New Zealand
{brian.cusack,zhuang.tian}@aut.ac.nz
[2] Facuty of Business and Information Technology, Whitireia Community Polytechnic – Auckland Campus, 450 Queen Street, Auckland, New Zealand
arkar.kyaw@whitireia.ac.nz

Abstract. Society is faced with the ever more prominent concerns of vulnerabilities including hacking and DoS or DDoS attacks when migrating to new paradigms such as Internet of Things (IoT). These attacks against computer systems result in economic losses for businesses, public organizations and privacy disclosures. The IoT presents a new soft surface for attack. Vulnerability is now found in a multitude of personal and private devices that previously lacked connectivity. The ability to trace back to an attack origin is an important step in locating evidence that may be used to identify and prosecute those responsible. In this theoretical research, IP traceback methods are compared and evaluated for application, and then consolidated into a set of metrics for potential use against attackers.

Keywords: Attack origins · DoS · DDoS · TTL · Traceback · IoT security

1 Introduction

A Denial of Service (DoS) attack can be characterized as an attack with the purpose of preventing legitimate users from using some specific network utilities such as a website, web service or computer system [1]. On the other hand, a Distributed Denial Service (DDoS) attack is a coordinated attack on the availability of the service of a given target system or network. It is launched indirectly through many compromised computing systems. The websites used to launch the attack are often called the '*secondary victims*' [2]. The use of secondary victims in a DDoS attack provides an attacker with the ability to launch a much larger and more disruptive attack than a DoS attack while remaining anonymous since the secondary victims actually complete the attack making it more difficult for the digital forensic investigator (DFI) to track down the original attacker. In general, there are two types of flooding attacks [3]: direct and reflector attacks. In a direct attack, an attacker sends a large number of attack packets directly towards the victims. Attack packets can be of Transmission Control Protocol (TCP), Internet Control Message Protocol (ICMP), User Datagram Protocol (UDP) or a mixture of them,

© ICST Institute for Computer Sciences, Social Informatics and Telecommunications Engineering 2017
N. Mitton et al. (Eds.): InterIoT 2016/SaSeIot 2016, LNICST 190, pp. 127–138, 2017.
DOI: 10.1007/978-3-319-52727-7_14

for example Internet Protocol (IP) flooding [4], Synchronization (SYN) flooding [5, 6]. A reflector attack is an indirect attack in those intermediary nodes (routers and various servers), also known as '*reflectors*', are innocently used as attack launchers [7]. An attacker sends packets that require responses to the reflectors with the packets' inscribed source addresses set to a victim's address. Without realizing that the packets are actually address spoofed, the reflectors return response packets to the victim according to the types of the attack packets. As a result, the attack packets are essentially reflected in the form of normal packets towards the victim. Consequently, the reflected packets can flood the victim's network if the number of reflectors is large enough.

One reason that spoofing is often facilitated in these and other DoS or DDoS attacks is that it allows evasion of filters and quotas based on sender IP address, making tracing attackers harder [2, 8] reinforce that tracking back attack origin in DDoS attacks is a difficult and non-trivial problem due to the following reasons. Firstly, it is easy to forge or modify IP address (e.g. IP spoofing). Secondly, the stateless nature of IP routing, where routers normally know only the next hop for forwarding a packet instead of the entire end to end path taken by each packet, makes IP traceback even harder. Moreover, the Internet was originally designed for fast file sharing in a trusted environment and the network security was less important than communications, as it was a secondary consideration. Routers do not verify the source address of IP packets and the entire routing table is constructed on a trust basis. However, the wide adoption of these limitations with the dramatic increase of users, attackers can easily exploit IoT vulnerabilities to launch attacks.

[9] state that there are three types of DDoS defense approach mechanisms depending on their locality of deployment. These are: source-end approach (i.e. the detection approach is implemented in the routers of attacker networks), victim-end approach (i.e. the detection approach is implemented in the routers of victim networks) and in-network approach (i.e. the detection approach is implemented in intermediary routers between victim and attacker networks). Detecting a DDoS attack at the victim-end is easy, but often not useful if it is not a real time detection. In-network solutions are not deployable in real network, unless the whole Internet infrastructure is changed. On the other hand, the source-end detection is a very challenging task as a malicious person can launch attacks from anywhere and anytime. So, the best possible practically deployable solution for DDoS attack detection can be a victim-end detection approach which detects attacks in real time while ensuring high detection accuracy. However, the degree of computational complexity for victim-end scheme has to be low in real-time detection. This might again adversely affect the performance in terms of detection accuracy. The ability to trace back to an attack origin is an important step in locating evidence that may be used to identify and prosecute those responsible. IP traceback is to find the origin of malicious attacking packets [10]. Since routers are the core connectivity devices that direct all traffic in the Internet, most of the IP traceback methods have routers in their design. These traceback methods were developed according to various situations and have their distinct features for tracing back to attack origins. Most of them depend on collecting a large number of packets from routers along the attacking path. Without collecting sufficient packets, tracing back is extremely difficult and sometimes impossible. These methods are also resource costly. The full stream of packets from the routers used to reconstruct the attacking path would be required. The objectives of this paper is to

compare and evaluate existing IP traceback methods, present challenges and provide research directions for future work. This paper is organized into five sections including the "Introduction (Sect. 1)", which is followed by a background literature review of traditional IP traceback methods (Sect. 2) to gain contextual knowledge. Section 3 presents the analysis of a number of recent IP traceback methods and limitations. Afterwards, we propose evaluation metrics for IP traceback methods (Sect. 4), which is followed by the conclusion and future work (Sect. 5).

2 Traditional IP Traceback Methods

IP traceback methods are developed and tested for determining the origin of a packet. Each method attempts to exploit technical possibilities in networks but each runs into difficulties. In general, the ability to consistently connect one network entity to another is lost in the architecture and dynamics of the networks. Multicast routing and many-to-many relationship of communications between networks prevent a single solution to fit all traceback requirements. Each attempt to provide a solution demonstrates the strengths and weaknesses of a preferred approach. Usually, unknown relationships (unicast or one-to-one, multicast or one-to-many, and broadcast or one-to-all) and interaction between network hosts (e.g. a web server and a web client) place limits on the effectiveness of any particular approach. Similarly, most of IP traceback methods developed so far have many serious flaws with falsified IP addresses or spoofing. These traditional traceback methods require an enormous number of packets in order to reconstruct malicious packet paths and demand more computational power, storage, deployment overhead, network throughput and effective response time. Hence, the disadvantages far outweigh the benefits and the overall performance does not seem to be sufficient.

Nowadays, most of IP traceback methods belong to five main categories such as link testing hop-by-hop tracing, ICMP messaging, logging, packet marking and hop count filtering [11]. These traceback methods are developed according to various situations and have their distinct features for tracing back to attack origins. Most of these methods depend on collecting a large number of packets from routers along the attacking path. In fact, a full stream of packets from the routers used to reconstruct the attacking path is required. As a result, these methods are also resource costly (Table 1).

Table 1. Traditional IP traceback methods analysis.

Traceback Scheme	Advantages	Disadvantages
Input Debugging [12]	• Using single packet analysis • Allowing post packet analysis • Can be used to against both DoS or DDoS • Bandwidth overhead is very low	• ISP cooperation is high • Time consuming is high • Not scalable for multiple DoS or DDoS attack at the same time • May require court approval

(continued)

Table 1. (*continued*)

Traceback Scheme	Advantages	Disadvantages
	• Storage requirement is very low • Computational overhead is very low • No functions needed to implement	
Controlled Flooding [13]	• ISP cooperation is not required • Easy to implement • Can be used to against DoS attack • Storage requirement is very low	• Time consuming is high • Substantial packets required • Bandwidth overhead i.e. it generates additional network traffics • Potentially, can be considered as a small DoS attack • Legal permission may be required • Can only be used during attack • Cannot distinguish DDoS and genuine flash crowed
ICMP [14–16]	• Compatible with existing protocols • Supporting incremental implementation • Allowing post packet analysis • ISP cooperation is not required • Compatible with existing routers and network infrastructure	• Bandwidth overhead i.e. it generates additional network traffic • Less protective as there is no encryption scheme implemented with key distribution
Logging [19–21]	• Compatible with existing protocols • Medium level of ISP cooperation is required • Allowing post packet analysis • Using single packet to reconstruct attack path • Easy to implement	• Substantial storage required • Have potential hash collision • Depending on data storage size and searching algorithms, extra searching time is required • Path reconstruction need to be completed before stored attacking packet being overwritten • Extra computational resources needed for intermedia routers • Reducing network throughputs
Packet Marking [12, 18]	• Low processing • Suitable for a variety of attacks • It does not have inherent security flaws	• Since every router marks packets probabilistically, some packets will leave the router without being marked • It is too expensive to implement this scheme in terms of memory overhead

(*continued*)

Table 1. (*continued*)

Traceback Scheme	Advantages	Disadvantages
	• It does not reveal internal topologies of the ISPs • It is scalable	• One important assumption for PPM to work is that DoS attack traffics will have large volume than normal traffic. However this assumption is not valid when attack is highly distributed for example in reflector attacks • High bandwidth overhead • Costing data fragmentation
Hop Count Filtering [23]	• Compatible with existing protocols • Easy to implementation • Compatible with existing routers and network infrastructure • Allowing post packet analysis • ISP cooperation is not required • Can be used to against both DoS or DDoS • It is feasible for wide deployment • It can be used to detect the attack even when it is over • Bandwidth overhead is very low • Storage requirement is very low	• It cannot identify the very first router, rather just give a possible list • It requires pre-generated map of the internet topology

3   Recent IP Traceback Methods

From the above evaluations, the traditional IP traceback methods have their own advantages and disadvantages. Quite often, they are cumbersome to implement. They either require high computational overhead, data storage or even introduce substantial extra packets on the Internet which can significantly reduce the overall network performance. None of the traditional IP traceback methods can provide high-level performance accuracy with cost-effective benefit. In the past decade, researchers [22, 24–26] have tried to invent several new IP traceback methods by combining/merging various traditional methods together in aiming to provide a fast-single packet traceback result. This section will compare and evaluate these IP traceback methods (Table 2).

Table 2. Recent IP traceback methods analysis.

Trace-back scheme	Advantages	Disadvantages
TTL & DPM [22]	• Suitable for a variety of attacks • It does not reveal internal topologies of the ISPs • It is scalable • Allowing post packet analysis • ISP cooperation is not required • It can be used to trace the attack even when it is over	• Resource incentive in terms of processing and storage requirements • Cannot be used to trace DDoS because DDoS may not generate the minimum amount of packets used for DPM • It is not feasible for wide deployment since it requires all the routers to mark the packet in certain percentage • Since every router marks packets probabilistically, some packets will leave the router without being marked • It is too expensive to implement this scheme in terms of memory overhead • Time consuming as extra encryption and decryption steps introduced
Marking & Logging [24]	• Compatible with existing protocols • Supporting incremental implementation • Allowing post packet analysis • Compatible with existing routers and network infrastructure • It is scalable • Provide single packet traceback capability	• Resource incentive in terms of processing and storage requirements • Sharing of logging information among several ISPs leads to logistic and legal issues • Less suitable for DDoS • Since every router logs packets probabilistically, some packets will leave the router without being logged • It is too expensive to implement this scheme in terms of memory overhead • It requires large packets to reconstruct attacking path
Hop Count & Marking [25]	• Suitable for a variety of attacks • It does not reveal internal topologies of the ISPs • It is scalable • Allowing post packet analysis • ISP cooperation is not required • Can be used to against both DoS or DDoS	• Resource incentive in terms of processing and storage requirements • Medium processing overhead is required • Since every router marks packets probabilistically, some packets will

(continued)

Table 2. (continued)

Trace-back scheme	Advantages	Disadvantages
	• It is feasible for wide deployment • It requires small number of packets to reconstruct attacking path	leave the router without being marked • It is too expensive to implement this scheme in terms of memory overhead
FDDA [26]	• Using features that are out of control of hackers to conduct IP traceback • It does not suffer from the problem of packet pollution • This model can work as an independent software module with the current routing software which helps in ease in implementation	• This technique does not consider the differentiation of DDoS attacks and flash crowds; it may treat flash crowd as DDoS attack resulting in false positive • It is impossible to determine the location of router • Poor performance

4 Proposed Evaluation Metrics for IP Traceback Methods

The analysis of traceback methods shows that each method uses different techniques to find the original source of attack and the potential location of the attackers. All methods have advantages and disadvantages. To evaluate different traceback methods, the Open Systems Interconnection (OSI) reference model provides an incremental measurement for expectations across the seven layers. The essential task of IP traceback is to find the origin of a particular IP packet traversing the Internet. OSI model can explain the communication expectation through each layer. Protocols serve as the building blocks for the Internet; and different protocols are specifically based on different layers of OSI model. Traceback methods exploit and explore these protocols. Thus, the OSI model also serves as a foundation for benchmarking traceback methods. For example, when data is passed down from layer 7 to layer 1 before being sent to the Internet from source device, each layer encapsulates the data with its header accordingly. These headers contain information about the data as well as the type of protocol being used in accordance with each OSI layer when the data is being passed. Conversely, when the encapsulated data arrives at the destination device, to allow a user to retrieve the information, the data is passed from the lowest layer to the highest layer on OSI model. Moreover, to process the data accordingly, a header will be stripped to enable an appropriated protocol at each layer and pass the remaining data to the level above until it reaches layer 7. The data then will be presented as information understood by user. Therefore, data encapsulated at a lower layer contains more information for traceback exploitation compared with data that has been encapsulated by the layer above. Thus, using the protocols at the lower layer, the more information can be retrieved from the encapsulated data. This also applies to traceback methods. The lower the layer of protocol being used by the traceback method, the more information can be used to find the source of the communication.

On the other hand, the backbone of the Internet consists of routers, switches and physical communication medium connecting all the components of the Internet.

Across different LANs, mostly routers at the Network Layer are processing data. Accordingly, this layer of encapsulated data is known as a packet. Though most proposed traceback methods use different protocols; yet they are all based on the Network Layer. Also, to effectively measure those methods, a set of evaluation metrics should be established. [2] suggest measurement criteria for IP traceback methods, and yet they lack accurate performance evaluation characteristics. Hence, we then propose the following evaluation metrics for IP traceback methods:

- **ISP involvement:** There are no incentives given to the ISPs and enterprise networks to monitor the attack packets and furthermore whether any ISP is involving in traceback method. An ideal traceback scheme should include minimum ISP involvement because the investigation may take longer time and more resources may be required with full co-operation.
- **The number of attacking packets needed for traceback:** IP traceback should able to traceback the attack source based on the packets when the attack has been identified. An ideal traceback scheme should be able to traceback the attacking source with one packet.
- **Processing overhead:** Additional processing overhead for measuring the flow of packets and calculating various statistical parameters are taken placed on the network devices like routers. An ideal traceback method should be able to incur minimal processing overhead during traceback.
- **Storage requirement:** Additional amount of memory is required to store certain information on the network devices to perform IP traceback. An ideal traceback method should be able to acquire a minimum amount of memory in network equipment.
- **Ease of implementation:** IP traceback algorithm is an important part of the solution for stopping DoS and DDoS attacks. These algorithms attempt to approximate the origin of the attack traffic. An ideal traceback method should be designed in such a way that it could be easily implemented at a network layer or application layer.
- **Scalability:** It refers to the amount of extra configuration required on the network devices when implementing a traceback method. An ideal traceback method should be scalable and independent from device manufacturers or vendors.
- **Bandwidth overhead:** Additional traffic that the network must carry for taceback is considered bandwidth overhead. Large bandwidth overhead is undesirable since it may exhaust the capacity of links and routers, forcing the ISP to introduce additional capacity and possibly upgrade or purchase new devices. An ideal scheme should not assume availability of infinite bandwidth.
- **Number of functions needed to implement:** This metric reflects how many different functions a vendor of equipment needs to implement for a given IP traceback method. It is easier for a vendor to implement fewer functions. Ideally, only a single function should be needed for implementation.
- **Ability to handle major DoS or DDoS attacks:** This is an extremely important metric that reflects how well the trackback method can perform the tracing of DoS or DDoS attack under severe circumstances (for instance; many attackers using reflectors or random address spoofing). However, many traceback methods are not able to cope with all types of attacks. An ideal scheme would be able to trace back all malicious attacks (Table 3).

Table 3. IP traceback methods comparison.

Traceback Method	Hop Count Filtering [23]	ICMP [14–16]	Logging [17, 19–21]	Packet Marking [12, 18]	Packet Marking & Logging [24]	TTL & Packet Marking [22]	FDDA [26]
ISP involvement	None	Low	Moderate	Low	None	None	None
No. of attack packets needed for traceback	1	Very Large	1	Very Large	1	Very Large	large
Processing overhead	Very Low	Low	Low	Low	Very Low	Low	High
Storage	Very Low	Low	Low	High	High	High	High
Ease of implementation	Yes	Yes	Yes	No	No	No	No
Scalability	Highest	High	Fair	High	High	Highest	Highest
Bandwidth overhead	None	Low	None	None	None	High	High
No. of functions needed to implement	3	2	3	2	5	5	6
Ability to handle major DDOS attack	Yes	Yes	Yes	Poor	Yes	Yes	Yes
Classification	IDS Based	Proactive	IDS Based	Proactive	IDS Based	Proactive	IDS Based
OSI model layer and protocols	IP, Network Layer	ICMP, Network Layer	IP, Network Layer	IP, Network Layer	IP, Network Layer	IP, Network Layer	IP, Network Layer

5 Conclusion

The review and analysis of traceback methods have been consolidated into a set of metrics that may be applied to enhance and improve the development of IP traceback methods. Many traditional traceback methods demonstrate limitations for practice. The theoretical deduction of solutions has not been enough to address practical problems that are found (for example, potential poor cooperation amongst ISPs). Other methods simply involve too much data that requires excessive storage and processing capabilities. Consequently, further research is required into the development of better algorithms and methodologies for optimizing the trace back to an attack origin. Attempts to mix and merge methods have been successful at reducing the overhead costs and approaching the origin more economically. However even with these more recent attempts at methodology improvement the ideal solution is not yet been established.

The wide adoption of IoT connectivity into people's daily lives everywhere has motivated the necessity of maintaining the integrity of communications. Initially, the Internet was designed for file sharing in a trusted environment. Security was of a lesser concern. Routers were designed so that they did not have to verify a sender's source IP address and the utility value of the internetworks was functionality. The more recent problem has been the exploitation of these global communication channels for criminal and terrorist purposes. Many of the advantages developed for efficient communication have been hijacked and are easy to exploit. For example, the vulnerability exploitation of DoS or DDoS attacks and the hiding of true IP addresses. These matters impact the integrity of IoT developments.

Another challenge is that most of the existing IP traceback methods are specifically designed for an Internet Protocol version 4 (IPv4) environment. However, IPv4 will become unsustainable in 2017 or 2018, and cannot meet the demand of IoT. IPv6 is capable for IoT and supports an IP address demand of 2^{128}. Currently, IPv6 packets are accounting for less than 2% of all Internet traffic. By far, only a few of research reports [27–30] are reported in IPv6 environment using the packet marking method. These proposed methods inherit the fundamental design flaws from the packet marking method reviewed in this paper. Thus, to design better performing traceback methods is urgent and a challenge for researchers for future work. This paper has contributed a consolidation of current literature and proposed a metric basis for further study.

References

1. Specht, S., Lee, R.: Distributed denial of service: taxonomies of attacks, tools and countermeasures. In: International Conference on Parallel and Distributed Computing Systems, pp. 543–550. San Francisco, CA, USA: CiteSeerX (2004)
2. Kumar, K., Sngal, A., Bhandari, A.: Traceback techniques against DDoS attacks: a comprehensive review. In: 2011 2nd International Conference on Computer and Communication Technology (ICCCT), pp. 491–498. IEEE, Allahabad, India (2011)
3. CERT Coordination Center.: Cert Advisories: CA-2000-01 denial of service developments. CERT Software Engineering Institute. http://www.cert.org/historical/advisories/ca-2000-01.cfm (2015)
4. Chen, T., Tsai, J., Gerla, M.: QoS routing performance in multihop, multimedia, wireless networks. In: IEEE 96th International Conference on Universal Personal Communications Record, vol. 2, pp. 557–561. IEEE, San Diego (1997)
5. Eddy, W.: TCP SYN flooding attacks and common mitigations, RFC4987. IETF: https://tools.ietf.org/html/rfc4987 (2007)
6. Lemon, J.: Resisting SYN flood DoS attacks with a SYN cache. In: 2nd European BSD Conference, pp. 89–98. Amsterdam, The Netherlands: USENIX (2002)
7. Paxson, V.: An analysis of using reflectors for distributed denial-of-service attacks. ACM SIGCOMM Comput. Commun. Rev. 31(3), 38–47 (2001)
8. Gilad, Y., Herzberg, A.: LOT: a defense against IP spoofing and flooding attacks. ACM Trans. Inf. Syst. Secur. 15(2), 6 (2012)

9. Kashyap, H., Bhattacharyya, D.: A DDos attack detection mechanism based on protocol specific traffic features. In: Proceedings of the Second International Conference on Computational Science, Engineering and Information Technology, CCSEIT 2012, pp. 194–200. ACM, New York (2012)

10. Yao, G., Bi, J., Vasilakos, A.: Passive IP traceback: disclosing the locations of IP spoofers from path backscatter. IEEE Trans. Inf. Forensics Secur. 10(3), 471–484 (2015)

11. Ho, C.: Email forensics: tracing and mapping digital evidence from my address. Unpublished Master's Thesis (2010)

12. Savage, S., Wetherall, D., Karlin, A., Anderson, T.: Network support for IP tracback. IEEE/ACM Trans. Netw. 9(3), 226–237 (2001)

13. Burch, H., Cheswick, B.: Tracing anonymous packets to their approximate source. In: Proceedings of the 14th USENIX conference on System Administration, LISA 2000, pp. 319–328. Berkeley, CA, USA: USENIX Association Berkeley (2002)

14. Bellovin, S.: ICMP Traceback Messages. Internet Draft: draft-bellovin-itrace-00.txt (2002)

15. Lee, H.C.J., Thing, V.L.L., Xu, Y., Ma, M.: ICMP traceback with cumulative path, an efficient solution for IP traceback. In: Qing, S., Gollmann, D., Zhou, J. (eds.) ICICS 2003. LNCS, vol. 2836, pp. 124–135. Springer, Heidelberg (2003). doi:10.1007/978-3-540-39927-8_12

16. Izaddoost, A., Othman, M, Rasid, M.: Accurate ICMP traceback model under DoS/DDoS attack. In: Proceedings of the 15th International Conference on Advanced Computing and Communications, ADCOM 2007, pp. 441–446. IEEE Computer Society, Washington, DC, USA (2007)

17. Sager, G.: Security fun with OCxmon and cflowd. Presentation at the Internet 2 Working Group (1998)

18. Song, D., Perrig, A.: Advanced and authenticated marking schemes for IP traceback. In: Proceedings of Twentieth Annual Joint Conference of the IEEE Computer and Communications Societies, INFOCOM 2001, vol. 2, pp. 878–886. IEEE, Anchorage, AK, USA (2001)

19. Snoeren, A., Partridge, C., Sanchez, L., Jones, S., Tchakountio, F., Schwartz, B., Kent, S., Strayer, W.: Single-packet IP traceback. IEEE/ACM Trans. Netw. 10(6), 721–734 (2002)

20. Ponec, M., Giura,P., Brönnimann, H., Wein, J.: Highly efficient techniques for network forensics. In: Proceedings of the 14th ACM Conference on Computer and Communication Security, CCS 2007, pp. 150–160. ACM, New York (2007)

21. Sung, M., Xu, J.J., Li, J., Li, L.E.: Large-scale IP traceback in high-speed internet: practical techniques and information-theoretic foundation. http://www.cc.gatech.edu/~mhsung/pub/ddos_sp.pdf (2008)

22. Devasundaram, S.: Performance evaluation of a TTL-based dynamic marking scheme in IP traceback. University of Akron, Akron (2006)

23. Wang, H., Jin, C., Shin, K.: Defense against spoofed IP traffic using hop-count filtering. IEEE/ACM Trans. Netw. 15(1), 40–53 (2007)

24. KrishnaKumar, B., Kumar, P., Sukanesh.: Hop count based packet processing approach to counter DDoS attacks. In: International Conference on Recent Trends in Information, Telecommunication and Computing (ITC), pp. 271–273. IEEE, Kochi (2010)

25. Yang, M., Luo, J.: High accuracy and low storage hybrid IP traceback. In: 2014 International Conference on Computer, Information and Telecommunication Systems (CITS), pp. 1–5. IEEE, Jeju (2014)

26. Park, P., Yi. H., Hong, S., Ryu, J.: An effective defense mechanism against DoS/DDoS attacks in flow-based routers. In: The 8th International Conference on Advances in Mobile Computing and Multimedia, pp. 442–446. ACM, Paris (2010)

27. Dang, X., Albright, E., Abonamah, A.: Performance analysis of probabilistic packet marking in IPv6. Comput. Commun. **30**(16), 3193–3202 (2007)

28. Michiko, H., Naoyuki, K., Daisaku, T.: Implementation of probabilistic packet marking for IPv6 traceback. IPSI BgD Trans. Internet Res. **1**(1), 54–58 (2005)

29. Amin, S., Hong, C., Kwak, D., Lee, J.: IPv6 traceback using policy based management system. Korean Netw. Oper. Manag. **9**(2), 1–7 (2006)

30. Yan, Q., He, X., Ning, T.: An improved dynamic probabilistic packet marking for IP traceback. Int. J. Comput. Netw. Inf. Secur. **2**(2), 47–53 (2010)

Author Index

Printed in the United States
By Bookmasters